I0616611

Fretboard Secret Handbook

2nd Edition

For beginner intermediate

By **Scott Su**

Hard to memorize notes and scales on guitar?

「Image Memory Method」!

TABLE OF CONTENT

Download Demo Tracks MP3 : scottsu.net/download

THE PRACTICE

THE APPLICATIONS

FOREWORDS

Regardless of types of music repertoire you want to play, if you don't know the actual position of each musical note, even it is playing an easy song like "Light Row", you would not know how to start playing it, and not to mention getting further to any advanced playing, or achieving the playing at ease as well as improvisations.

For friends who would like to try beginner's guitar, if you have an experience in learning other musical instruments, after reading this method book, you then can be faster in learning the guitar at ease. And it would be probably all right for you not to read a tablature. However, if you have no experience in learning other musical instruments at all, after reading this handbook, you then certainly can be faster in knowing reasons of pressing on those frets. This is very helpful to later continuations in advance playing.

For friends who are of intermediate level in their guitar playing, if you have a basic performance ability, but then you don't know what to do to allow yourself to be raised to an advanced level. Or you would like to re-arrange music you like, to create your own works but you feel your abilities are quite limited that you don't even know how to start with musical notes. This book then, can definitely help you.

If you wish to be roaming on a fretboard as wish, regardless of what music styles you would like to continue to learn or how strong your techniques are, still, you will need to ask yourself "Frankly, how familiar I am with the fretboard?", especially if you are quite interested and have set a learning goal in Jazz and Fusion music. Therefore, if you are not familiar with the fretboard, then you will feel very limited in just learning it, and this can affect your willingness and persistency in learning.

In this handbook, we mainly use a natural scale of a fixed key as a basic goal of familiarity. This is because it also represents your familiarity with positions of seven absolute pitch names of C D E F G A B on a fretboard, however, if you are not efficiently good at the distribution of the positions, then how are you going to improvise or even to compose? When you are very familiar with every position of musical notes on a fretboard, you will find the angle and even the image for you to view the fretboard to be different. The distribution picture of musical notes will look like graphic layers in Photoshop piling up on a fretboard. When you practice for a better familiarity, you then can be able to switch to different fingering graphics of different keys instantly. And in the end, even if you don't have the images in your eyes, your fingers then will know what positions of musical note to play next.

Some people may feel to say that why use a memorization method? Anyways, it is all about practicing scales non-stop, and we would get to memorize it slowly.

Certainly I personally also used this ancient type of method to practice on a fretboard before; however, one day when I didn't have a guitar in hand and I tried to use pen and paper to draw a fretboard and scales. Surprisingly, I discovered the rules of this picture. And thus, I applied them onto a guitar and all the sudden, I felt the distributions of musical notes on the entire fretboard appearing to be very clear visually. This is very helpful to playing and improvisation! After teaching my students these methods, they are all able to apply them with a good control for all positions of musical notes in just a few minutes as well as for their later practices on chords and scales. The students become more efficient in what they are doing. It is like in our childhood time, we learned to recite a multiplication table. Knowing its principles and then memorize the results directly. By doing so then, it is all very helpful no matter it is learning mathematics or to obtain better convenience in real life. Certainly our focus is on learning music, and graphics and images are very good methods of assistance. By helping finger muscles, we can quickly respond to positions of musical notes, in the end however, please remember to allow music and your ears to lead the fingers!

Regardless of what your goals for guitar are, being familiar with a fretboard is a necessary stage. So let's begin!

Scott

AUTHOR

Scott Su, an independent music composer, producer and guitarist from Taiwan. He is also a richly-experienced studio musician, skillful in music arrangements and releases mainly guitar performance albums. His self-composed albums include "_Are You Still There?_", a guitar performance single and "_No Flowers On Island_." Scott also writes useful guitar method books which include "_Fretboard Secret Handbook_" , "_Playing Guitar So Easy_", "_Your Training Notebook On Pop Music Special Chord Progressions_" and "_Your Personal Book Of Solo Fingerstyle Blues Guitar_ ".

✈ Site: https://ScottSu.net/

"_Are You Still There_"
A new acoustic guitar single
Composer / Arrangement / Recording / Mixing: Scott Su

"_No Flowers On Island_"
Electric / Acoustic Guitar Album
Composer / Arrangement / Recording / Mixing: Scott Su

Scott's Guitar Book Series

Playing Guitar So Easy

Learn the basic of song melody solo, singing accompaniment, fingerstyle song playing in a simple way !

Your Training Notebook on Pop Music Special Chord Progressions

Listen to the uniqueness, learn the harmony techniques, make your song become unique too !

Your Personal Book of Solo Fingerstyle Blues Guitar

Various types of theme-oriented Blues trainings on melody, harmony, rhythms and fingerstyle,...more diverse and rich Blues playing !

Chapter ONE

Building Blocks For Natural Scale

The distribution graphic of musical notes on the guitar is formed basically of two reasons:

1. Tuning

About the six strings of a guitar, under a standard tuning, starting from the thickest sixth guitar string is a low E, the fifth string is a low A, the fourth string is D, the third string is G, the second string is B and then to the first and the highest note E string. If we use a staff note to view this, it is like:

2. One half note is one fret

On a guitar fretboard, every move of one fret is a half note distance; two frets then, is a distance of one whole note.

For a natural major scale C D E F G A B, distance between the musical notes is as below (W=whole note; H=half note):

C (W) D (W) E (H) F (W) G (W) A (W) B (H) C

Hence, their distributions on the guitar become a graphic below:

THE FUNDAMENTALS : First, Clear Your Head

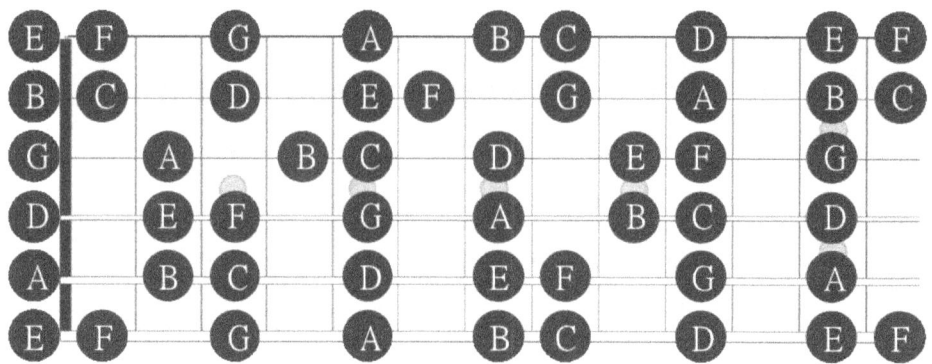

For a distribution graphic like this, in addition to the understanding and calculation of scales as well as continuous playing until you are familiar with the positions, what other methods do you think that can allow us to quickly memorize it?

Now we can use the most suitable pattern memorization method to help everyone memorize scale positions in a faster and more efficient way.

♦Patterns

First let's section the patterns in groups and from left to right, the grouping rules are:

<u>2 frets, 2 frets, 3 frets, 2 frets and 2 frets.</u>

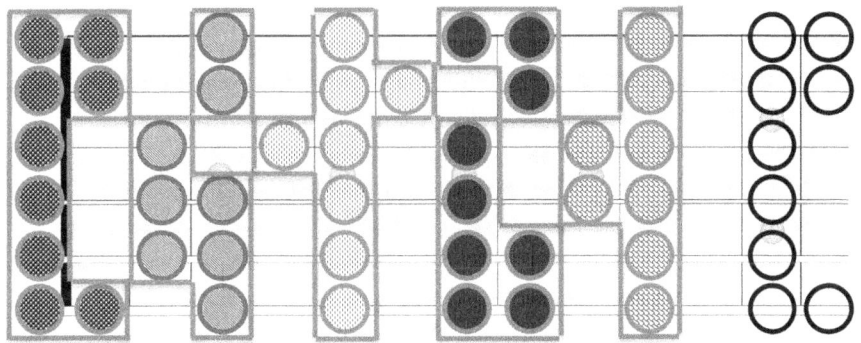

This way, every grouping pattern looks like building blocks! The concave and hollow of neighboring graphics are complementary, placing 5 pieces of graphic together then you will get a rectangular!

Now, first let's memorize 5 building blocks as well as their order from the left to right! Please try drawing this on your own on a piece of paper, and with more times of practice you can speed up the memorization. You then would tend not to forget it! (You can use the graphic above and directly draw circles to obtain the graphics.)

◆Pitch Names

The next step would be to figure out the pitch names of the musical notes on the memory building block graphic. There are two steps in this section:

1. <u>Gathering of Semitone</u>

It is a half step in between BC and EF, and they are gathering together on the guitar fretboard. It is only on the 2nd string and the 3rd string where one fret will be skipped.

Therefore, in the building block graphic, a square shape position, which is formed by EFBC 4 four notes, is as below:

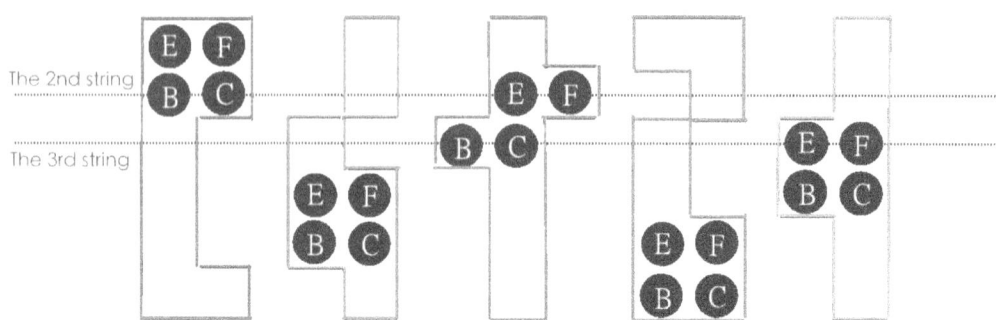

In the above graphic, there are two blank spaces for the 2 neighboring notes. If they are not EF then they would be BC, and what do you think they are? From standard tuning aspect, when the 1st string and the 6th string locate on the same fret, then it is the same pitch name. Therefore:

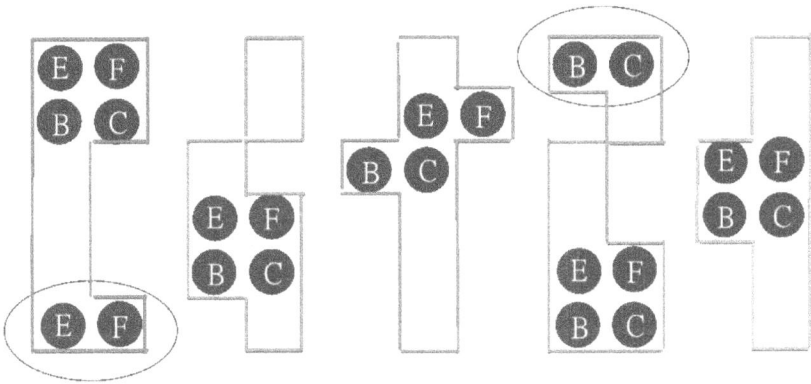

2. Arrangement of a Fourth Interval

After resolving 4 notes and the remaining blank spaces have ADG 3 musical notes to fill in. Similarly, by following the standard tuning, on the nearby string locating on the same fret, as long as you can remember using a perfect fourth interval to fill in, you may simply skip one fret when encountering the 3rd string entering to the 2nd string!

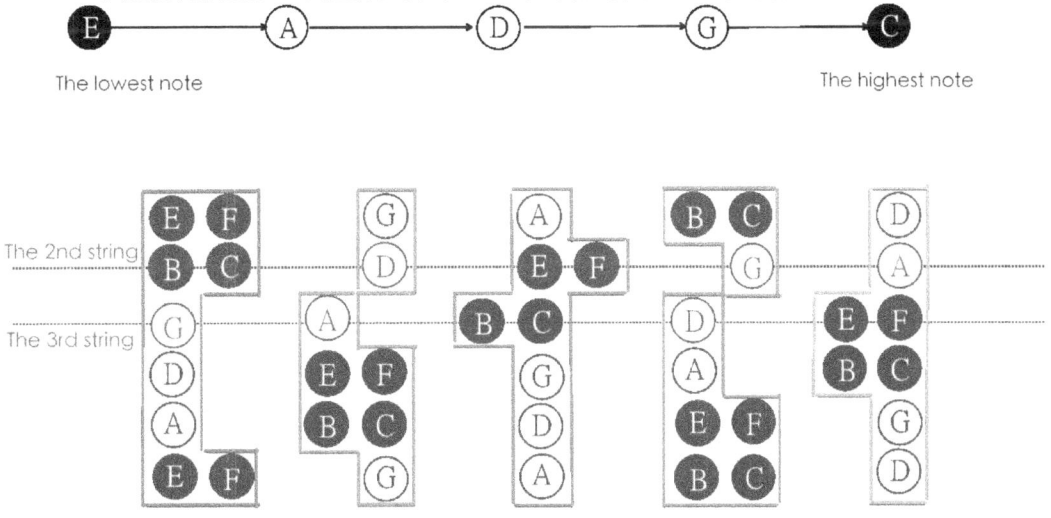

1. Five Pieces of Building Block Graphic

2. BCEF Gathering of Semitone

3. ADG Arrangement of a Fourth Interval

Therefore, in order to quickly memorize musical note positions on a fretboard, as long as you can follow the principles of these 3 steps to brainstorm, then you can quickly complete it. Even if you happen to forget, you can still quickly remember it, and the remaining would be done through more practices and hands-on to increase the familiarities of musical graphics!

■ Upon memorization, you would also need to see which number of frets is on the guitar. And this part can also be assisted with finger position marks on the fretboard.

♦ Explanations for Small Questions

☆ Why is it necessary to adjust one fret position when a musical note encounters the 2nd and the 3d strings ?

This is because the standard turning of guitar adopts a tuning of the neighboring 2 strings which equal to a distance of a perfect 4th interval, and only the distance between the 2nd and the 3rd strings is a major 3rd interval. What is between a major 3rd and a perfect 4th is one semitone difference. That is a distance of one fret. Therefore, the original musical note which is being developed based on a perfect 4th will still need to adjust one fret position when it is necessary.

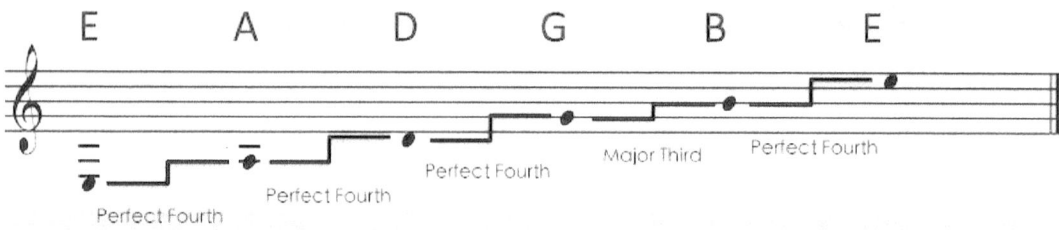

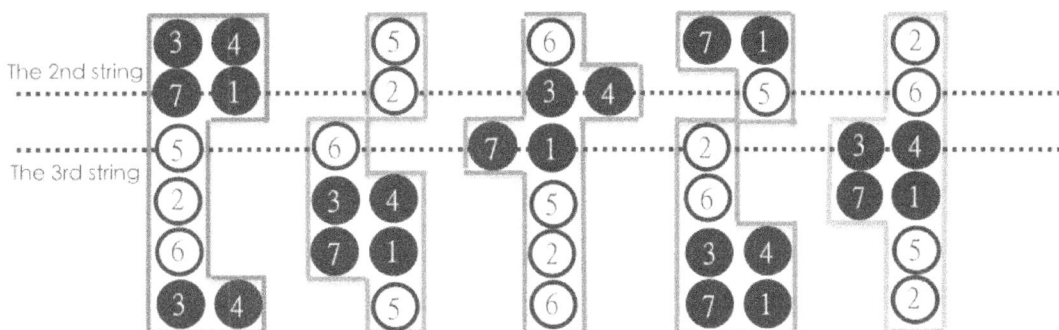

By switching to numbers of numbered musical notation can help us memorize tonic positions of different keys as well as the distributional relations between other musical notes on a scale.

♦ Natural Major vs. Natural Minor

Natural major key and minor key of the same key signatures use the same musical scales, therefore, their scale graphics are identical in presentation, and there's no need for additional memorization. As long as you can remember the tonic of a major scale is 1 in a scale (order of scale 1234567) , and the tonic of a minor scale is the 6th note (order of scale 6712345) in a scale, changes in an original order will cause changes in formats (Major—WWHWWWH, Minor—WHWWHWW) and it sounds differently aurally. Taking tonic of a minor scale as 1, according to a minor scale format it will be changed to 1 2 ♭3 4 5 ♭6 ♭7. So then you can see the differences comparing to a major key scale.

THE FUNDAMENTALS : First, Clear Your Head

♦Quiz

Please draw the remaining scale and tonic positions on a fretboard, and confirm it's a major key or a minor key (T represents tonic position).

(1)

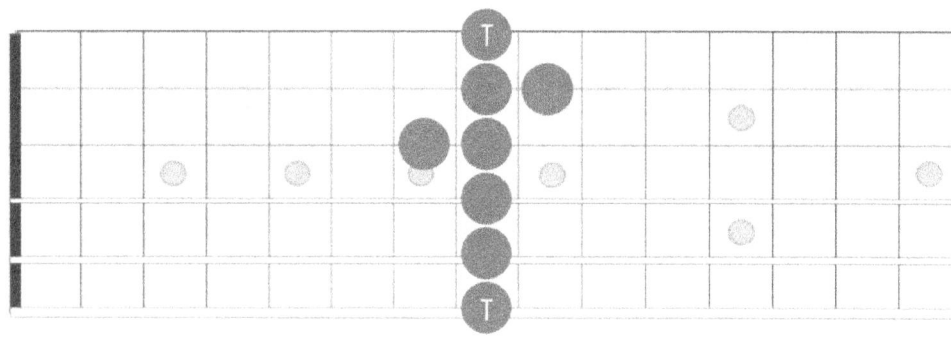

(2)

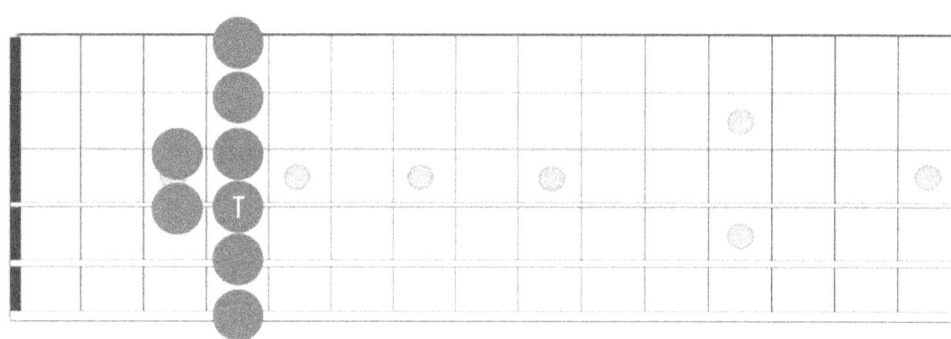

(3)

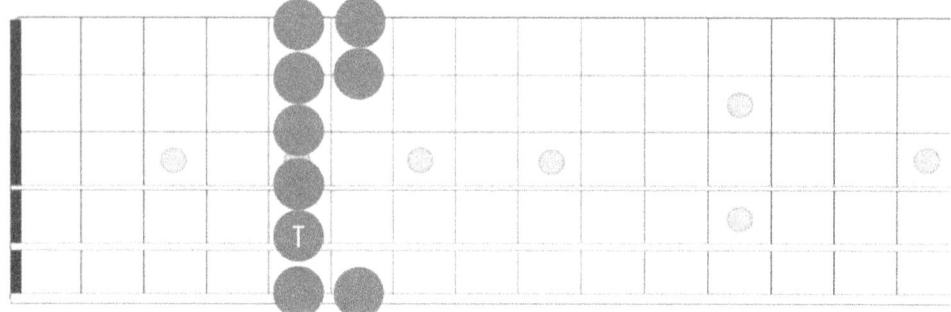

(4)

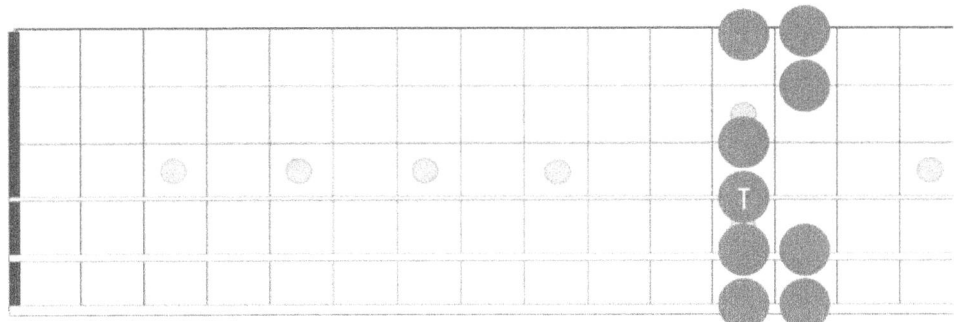

(5)

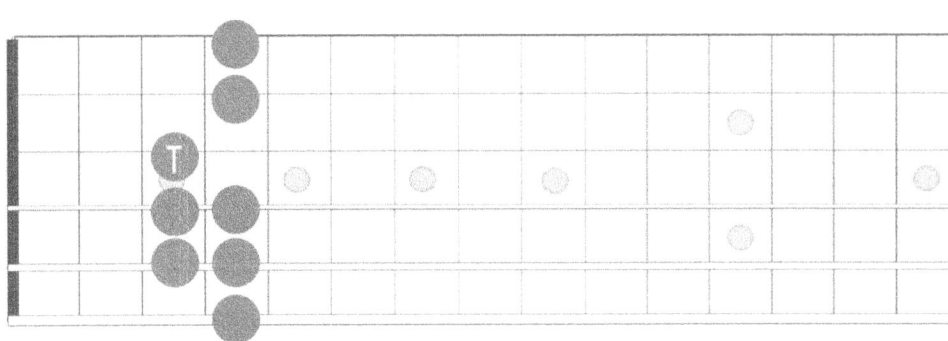

(6)

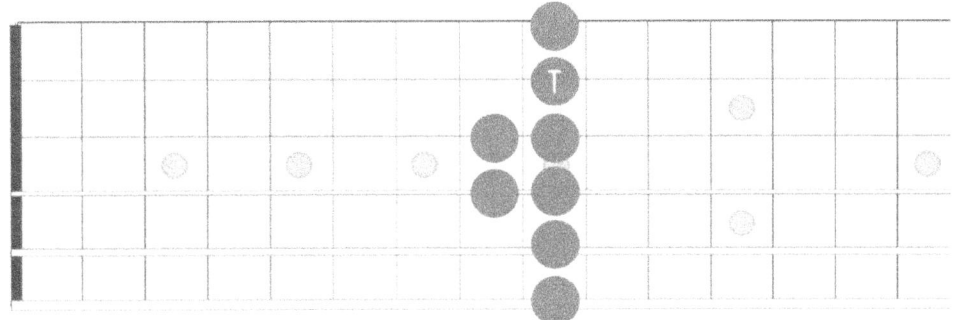

(7)

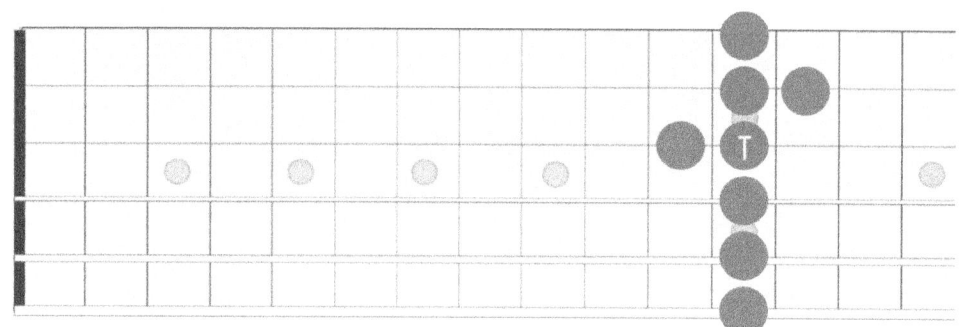

(8)

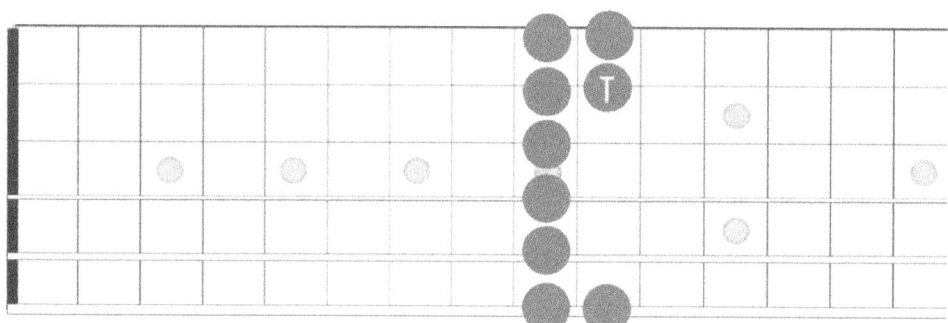

Chapter TWO

Position Graphic of Octave

The familiarity of an octave position can also help moving fret positions upon performance time. In addition to melodies, it is also quite helpful for quickly finding chord positions though!

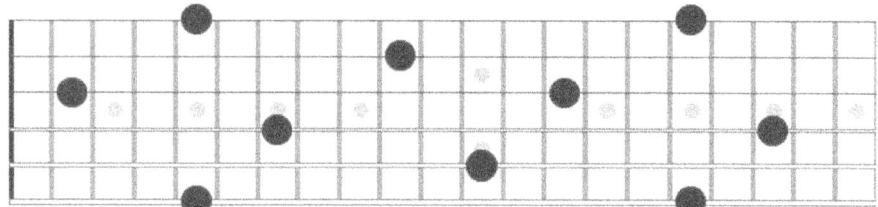

♦ Rules

1.   The identical fret of the 1st string and 6th strings is the same note, which has a two-octave difference.

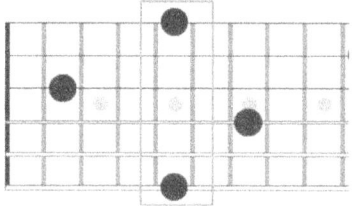

2.   Assuming you're looking for high octave notes towards a higher fret position:

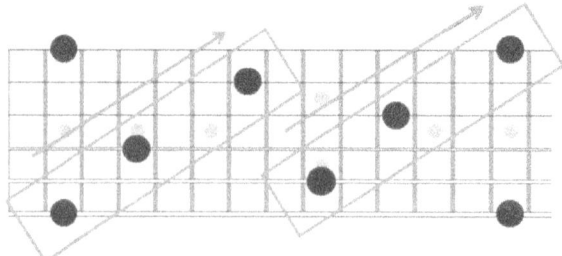

3.   Assuming you're looking for high octave notes towards a lower fret position:(Please pay attention to the set with the 6th string)

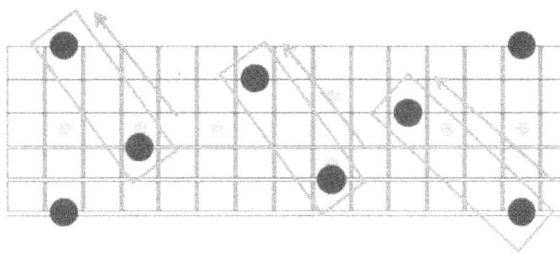

4.   Octave notes of the 1st string and 6th string can be viewed as a basic memory point via memorizing positions of octave note on both sides.

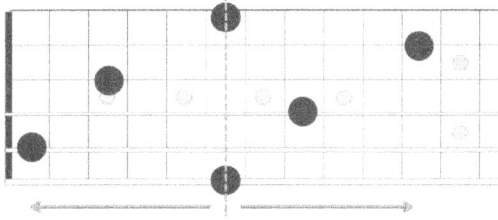

5.   High octave musical notes on each string:

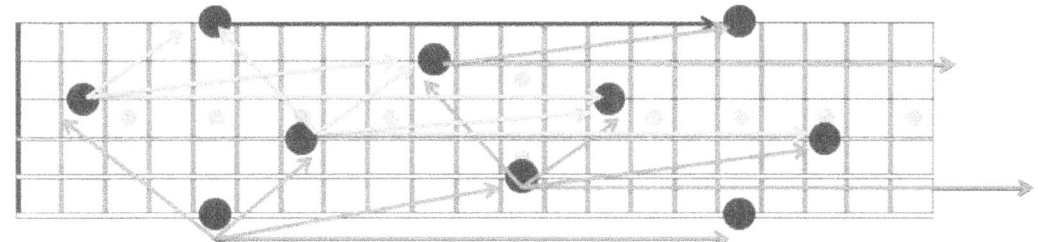

♦Quiz

Please find positions of other octave notes.

(1)

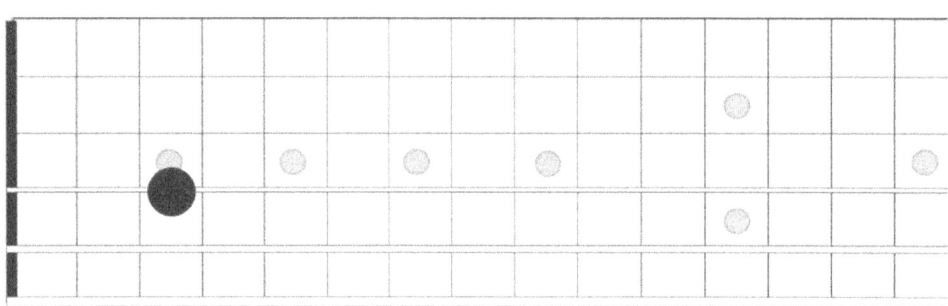

(2)

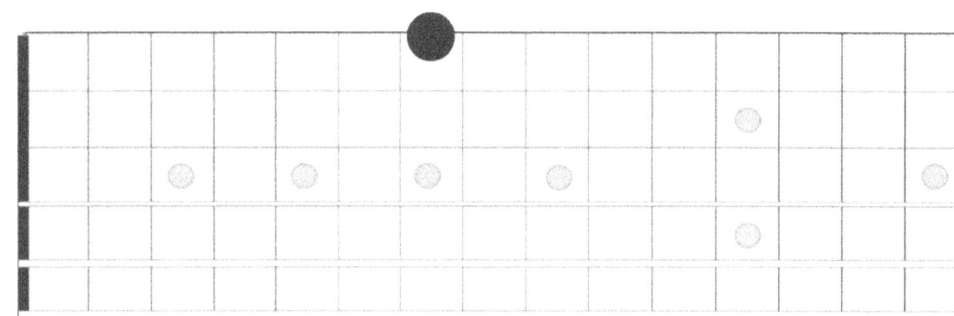

(3)

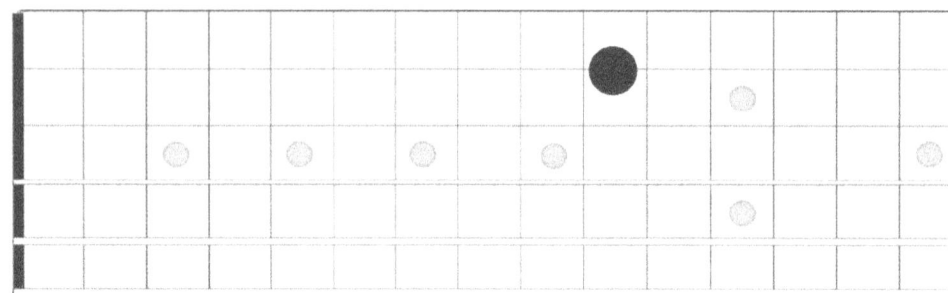

(4)

Chapter THREE

Other Relevant Scales Graphics

Next we would like to introduce other commonly-used scale graphics, which are transcribed from a natural scale. As long as we can follow a natural scale building block for musical note changes, then we won't mix them up with others.

◆Pentatonic Scale Graphic

It is simply to remove the 4th and 7th notes in natural scale. (Using the original 3471 square to eliminate 2 diagonal angles.)

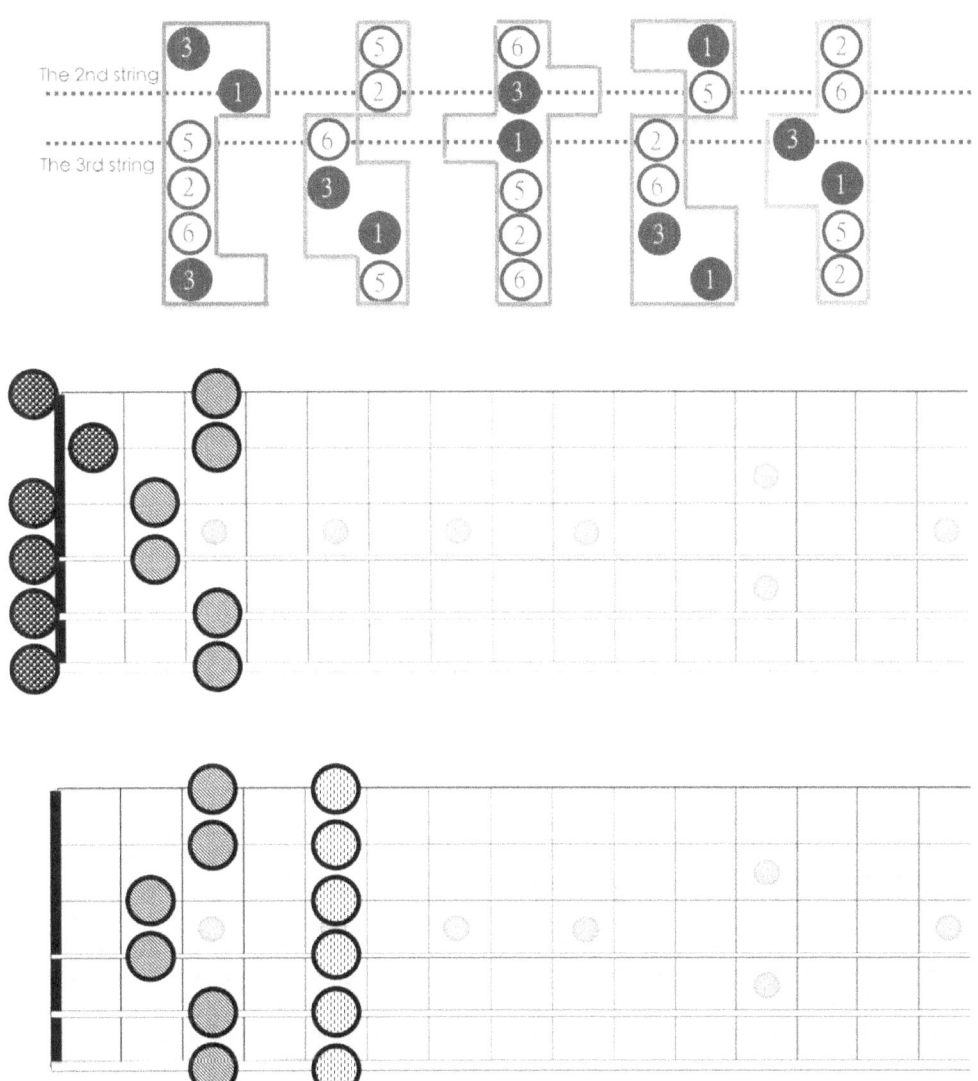

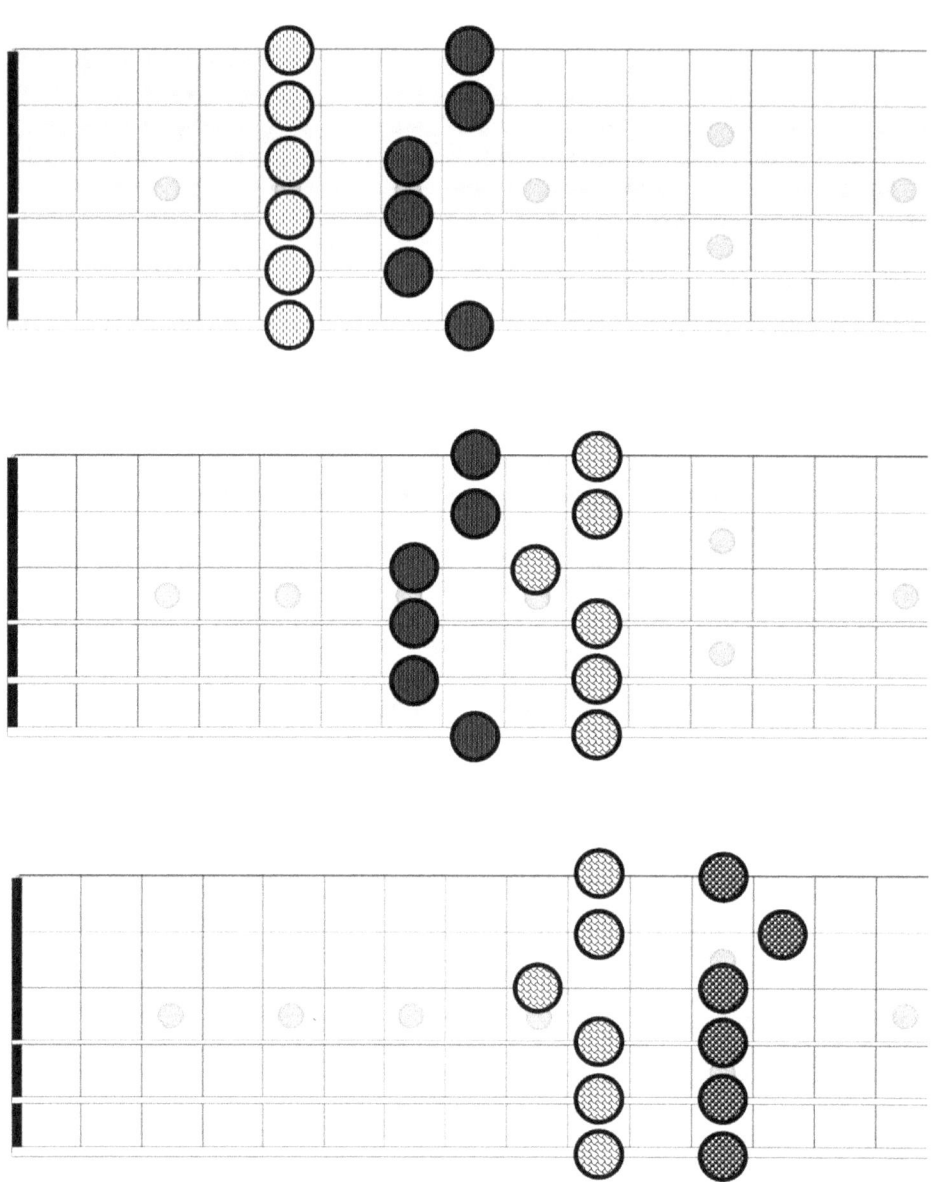

♦Quiz

Please draw the remaining positions of a pentatonic scale and a tonic on the fretboard, and also confirm whether it is a major key or a minor key.

(1)

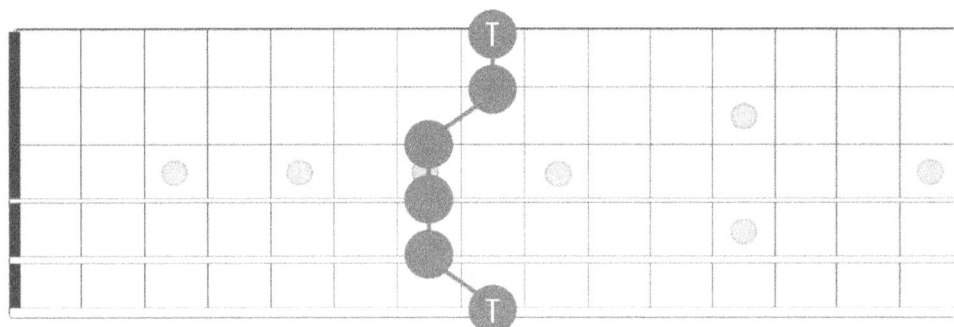

(2)

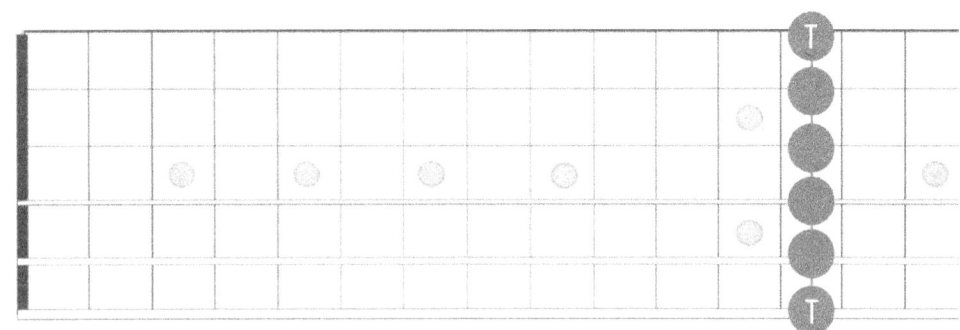

(3)

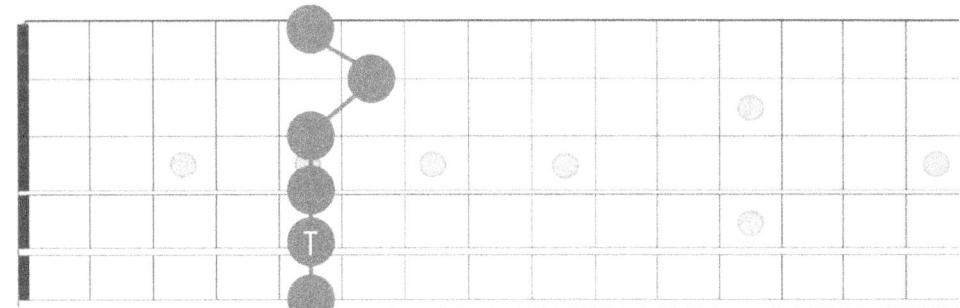

(4)

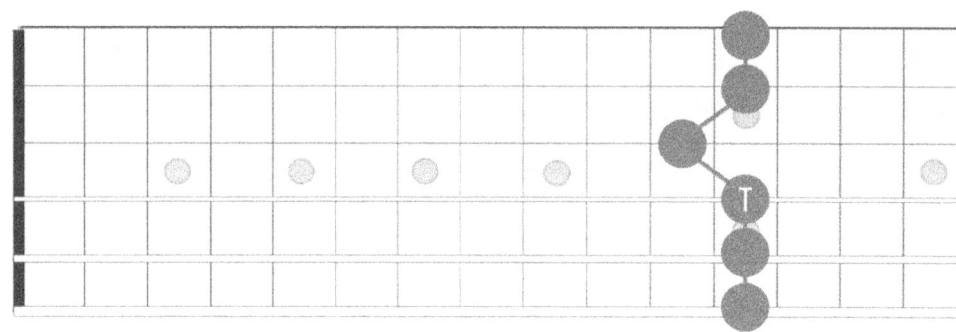

(5)

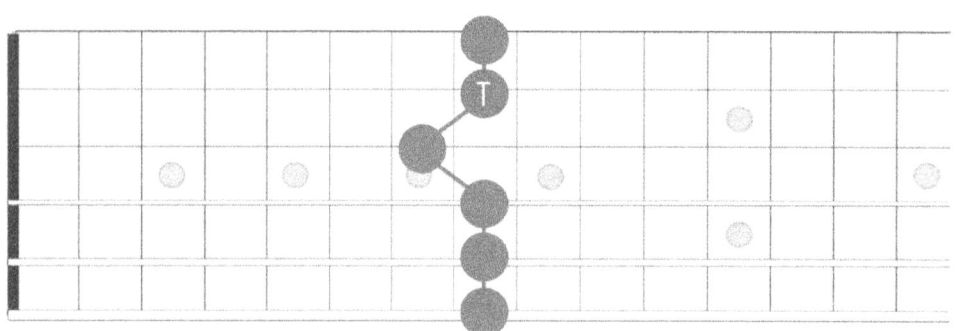

(6)

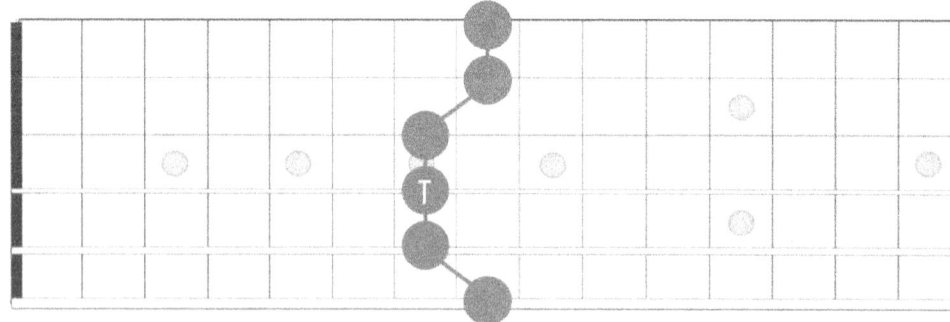

Tonic is 6, moving the 5th note in a natural scale ▶▶▶ #5 note is just fine.

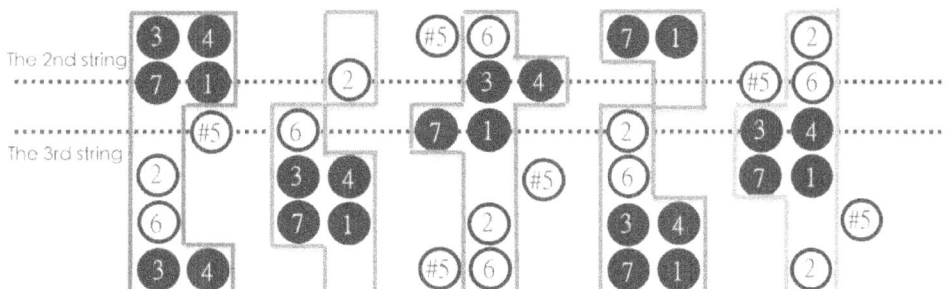

The tonic is 6, moving the 4th note in a harmonic minor scale ▸▸▸ $^{#}4$ is just fine.

(Attention: the descending direction of a melodic minor scale will become a natural minor scale, that is $^{#}4$ ▸▸▸4, $^{#}5$ ▸▸▸5, whereas Jazz minor scale will not be so.)

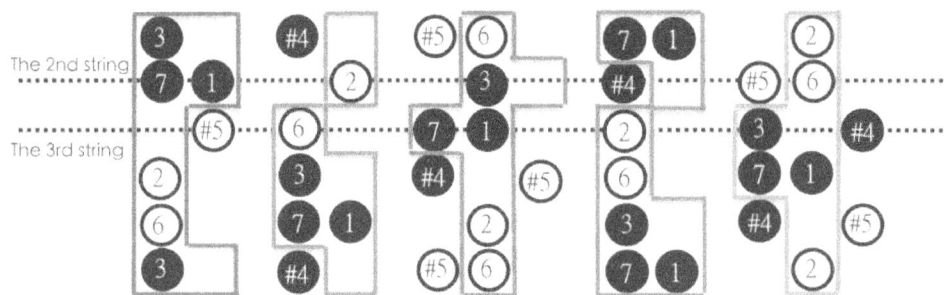

The general key mode scale refers to a European mode scale, and conceptually, it is about the same as major and minor scales. That is, to use the same natural scale, however, according to different tonic and then produces different order arrangement as well as format, and then the different aural effects. Because there are 7 comprising notes in a natural scale, there are 7 types of modal scale deriving from a natural scale. Similarly, 7 types of modal scale are derived from harmonic minor scale and melodic minor scale individually.

As conceptually, it is just the use of tonic in a scale to be different, so it is not necessarily to memorize a scale graphic. As long as you can practice it to be more familiar with the original 3 types of graphic, and please pay attention to that when a tonic is different, some unique acoustics of characteristic musical notes and chords, and then to further use it.

As for using modal scales for the familiarity of fretboard practices, please refer to chapter "Trainings On Modal Scale".

Tonic	Mode	Modal Scale	Scale Structure Format (Tonic is 1)
C	C Ionian	C D E F G A B	1 2 3 4 5 6 7
D	D Dorian	D E F G A B C	1 2 b3 4 5 6 b7
E	E Phrygian	E F G A B C D	1 b2 b3 4 5 b6 b7
F	F Lydian	F G A B C D E	1 2 3 #4 5 6 7
G	G Mixolydian	G A B C D E F	1 2 3 4 5 6 b7
A	A Aeolian	A B C D E F G	1 2 b3 4 5 b6 b7
B	B Locrian	B C D E F G A	1 b2 b3 4 b5 b6 b7

Chapter FOUR

"One String Three Notes" Scale Pattern Graphic

Patterns of "One String Three Notes" is for convenient and quickly proceeding to solo performance of a single note, and develop a type of fingering. According to the difference of starting note, there are additional 7 styles (Mi style, Fa style, Sol style ...). However, practically, you don't need to try too hard to memorize those seven graphics. In here, please allow me to tell you a faster and more efficient method to help you memorize this graphic.

♦Circulation Graphic of Natural Scale

<u>Graphic</u>

1. Firstly remember the easy graphics below:

 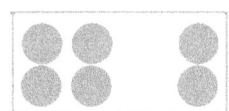 

2. And then understand their methods of circulation:

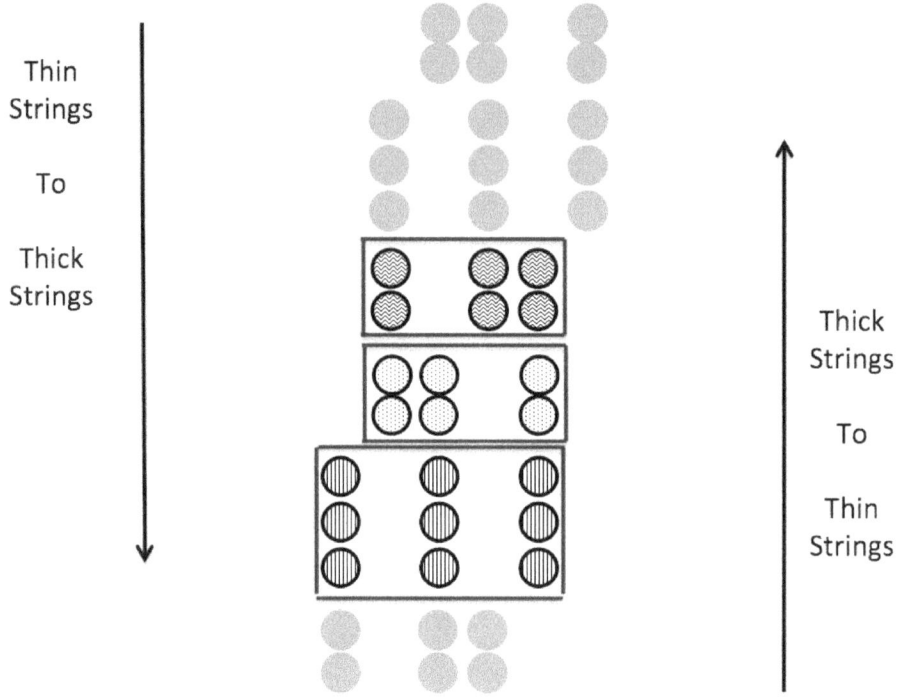

Thin Strings To Thick Strings

Thick Strings To Thin Strings

Methods of Use

The methods of use is that, whichever line in the graphics that you choose to start playing, as long as you follow the direction of circulation, please remember to adjust first fret position when encountering the 2nd string and the 3rd string, and then that's it!

After placing circulation graphic on the fretboard, you then can be clearer about the relation between every single type of fingering and the graphic!

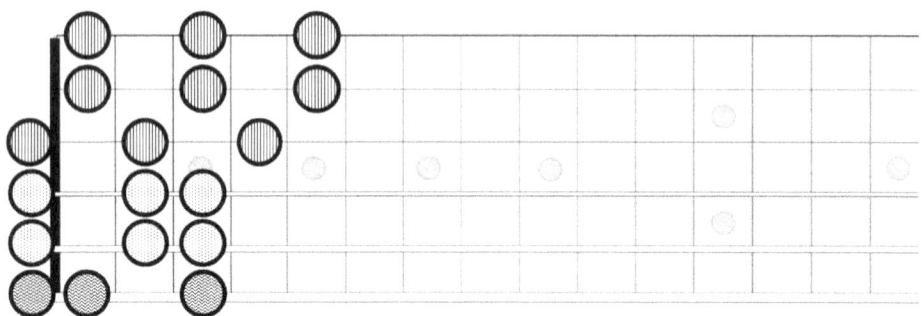

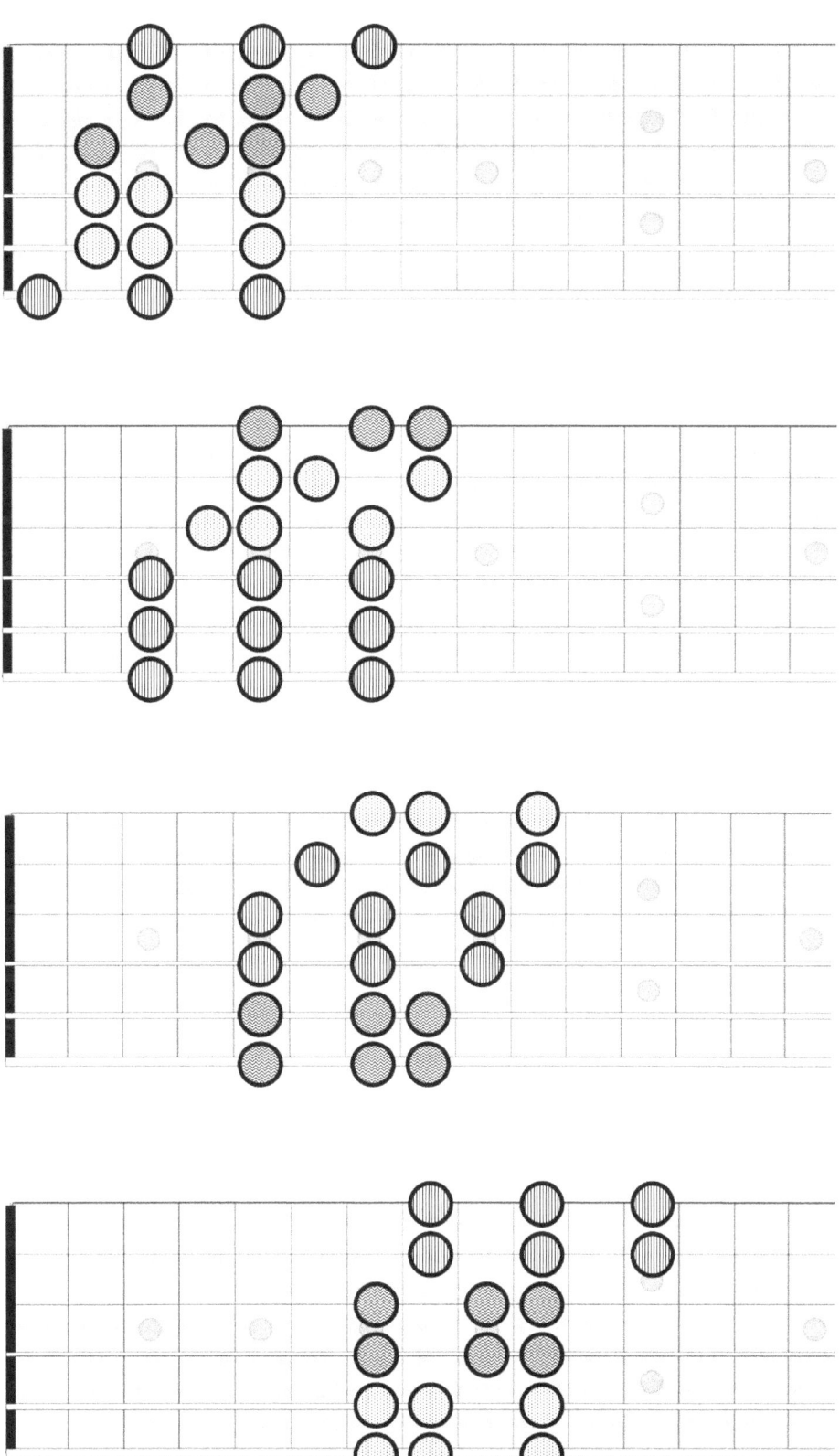

Pitch names

After there's no problem with the graphics, next you should be able to remember the musical notes in circulation graphic! Firstly, that is to fill in the four notes EFBC which can be gathered to form a square.

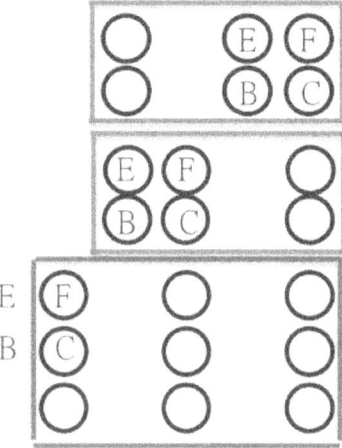

A circulation graphic has an assumption of a perfect fourth interval for the neighboring strings: therefore, the remaining musical notes are the same as what it has been explained in the building block graphic, or simply follow a scale order to fill in.

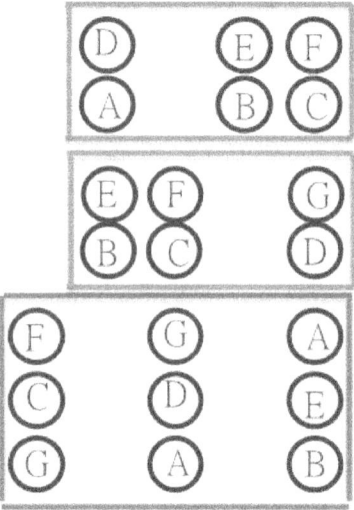

Transcribing to Numbers of Numbered Musical Notation

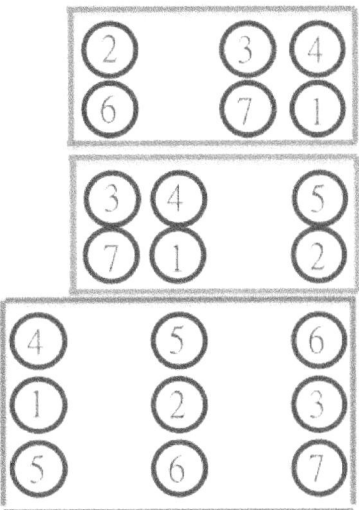

It is just like the building block graphic, please remember the tonic is 6, and then take 5 ▶▶▶ #5.

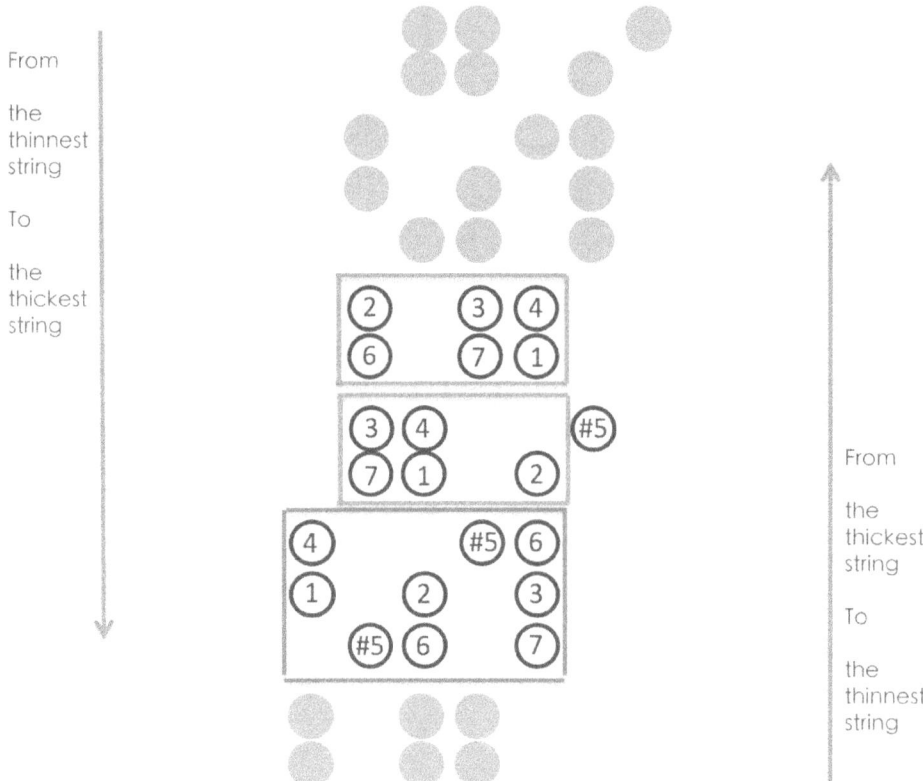

Circulation graphic of "One String Three Notes" on a fretboard:

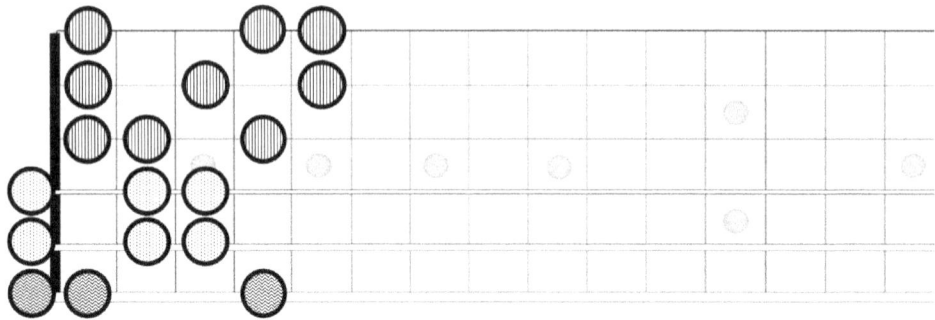

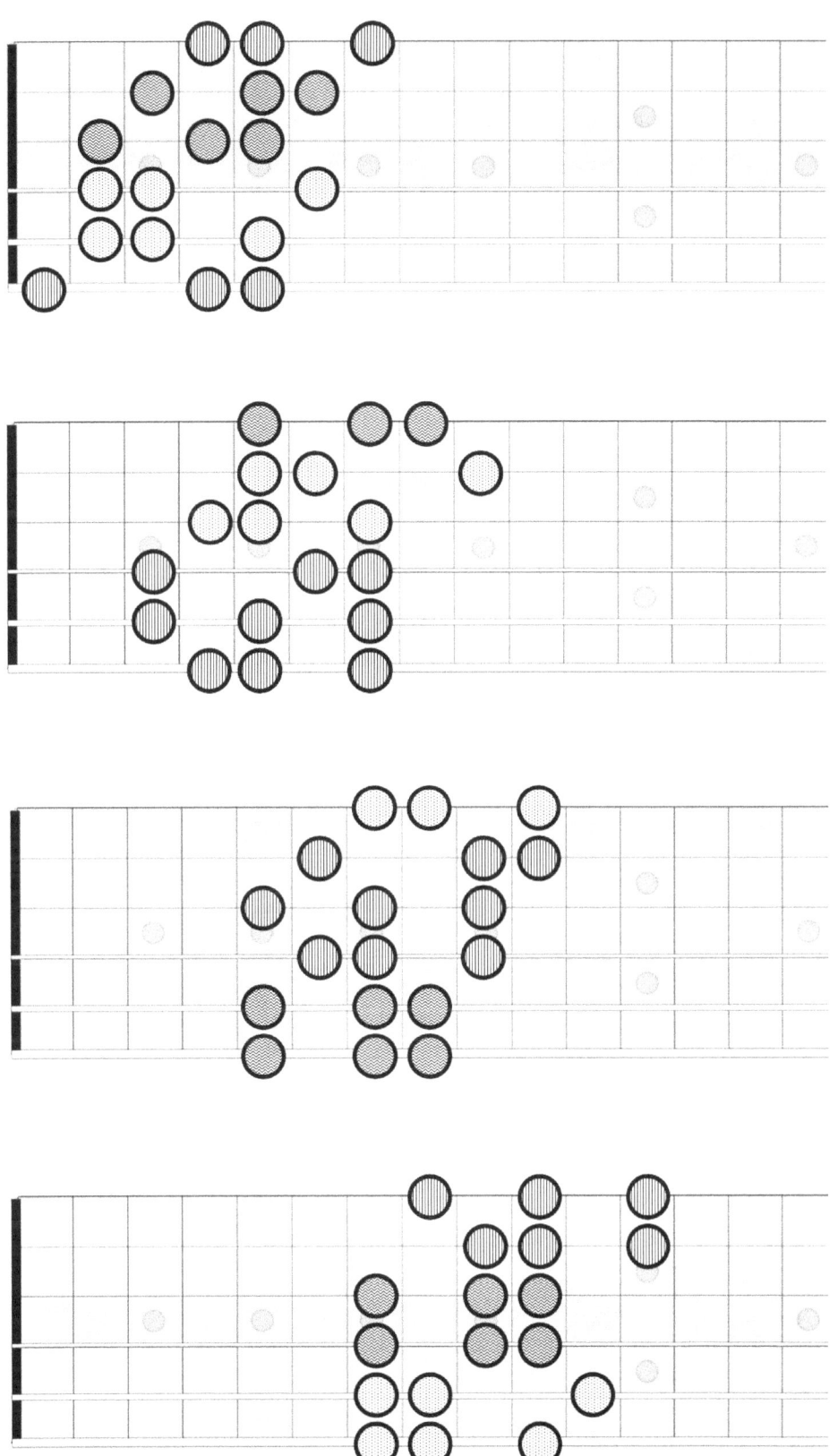

This is same as the building block graphic in which it uses 4 ▶▶▶ #4 of a harmonic minor scale. (Attention: the descending direction of a melodic minor scale will become a natural minor scale, and that is, #4 ▶▶▶ 4, #5 ▶▶▶ 5, whereas a Jazz minor scale will not be so.)

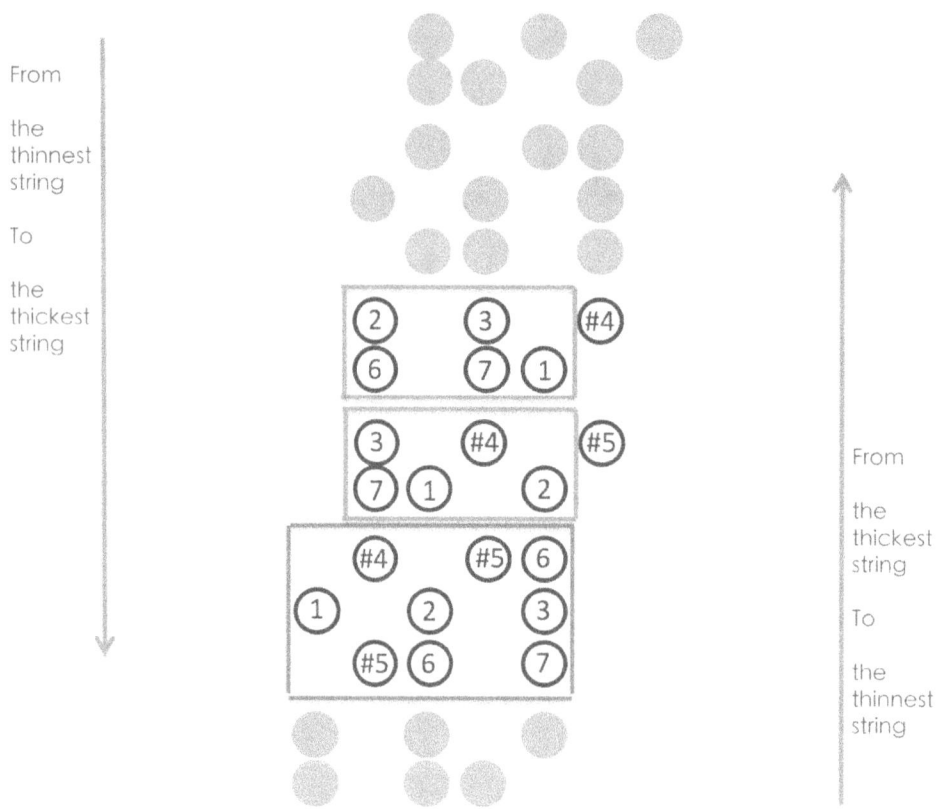

Circulation graphic of "One String Three Notes" on a fretboard:

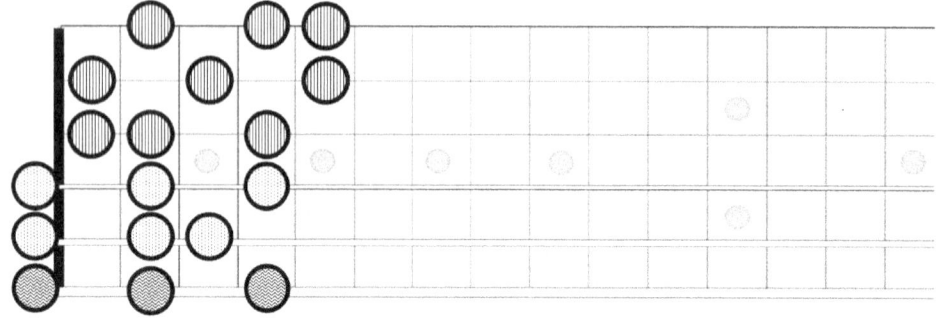

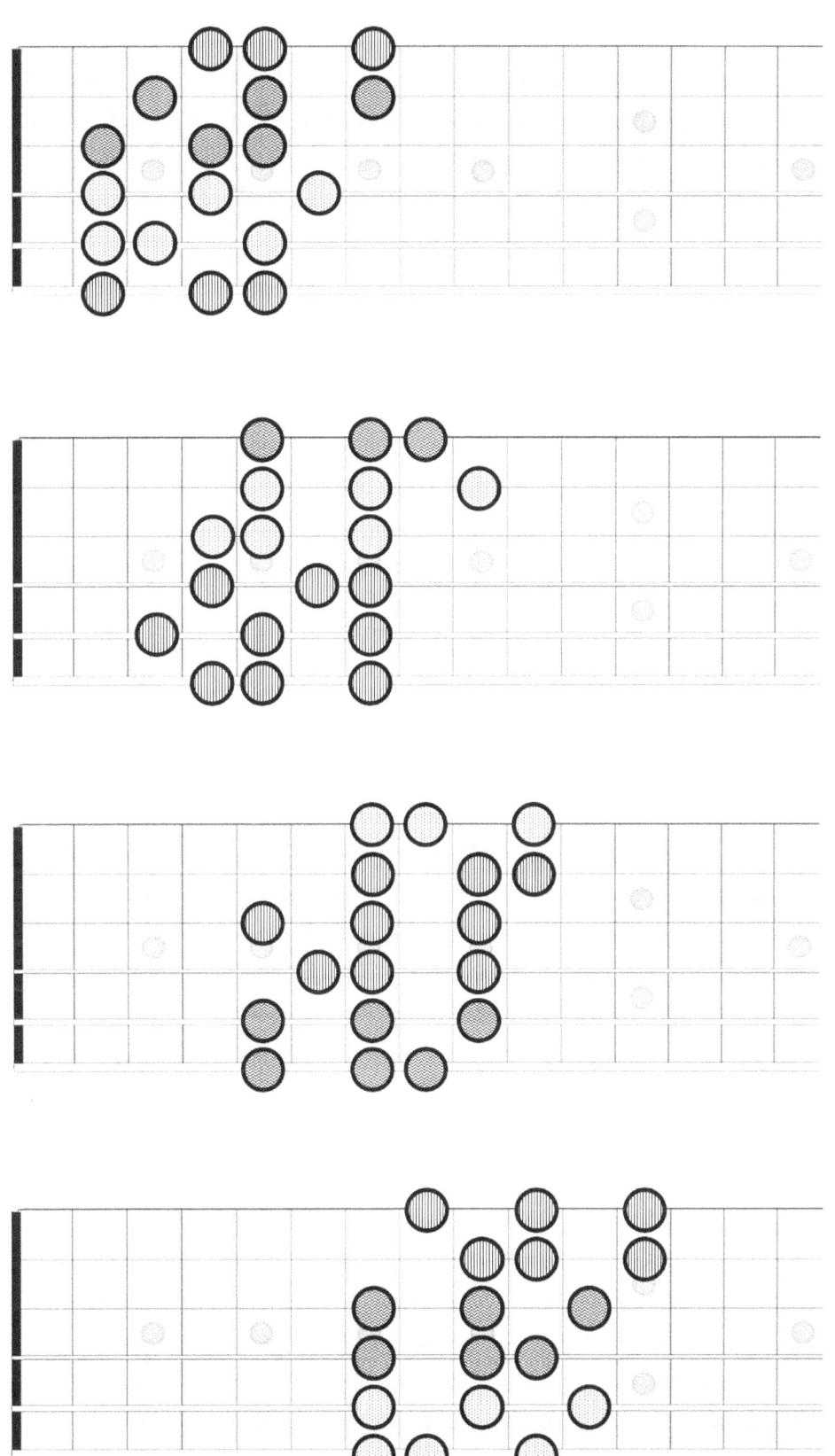

♦ Explanations for Small Questions

☆ Why do we need to memorize musical notes on different fret positions ?

This question may be of most keyboard players' question when they are learning the guitar. This is because in their thoughts, they would think that one musical note equals to one position. And in order to play a particular musical note, they would tend to find that particular position for playing the note.

Actually if you can think from the view of a keyboard, we can take the six strings of a guitar as an electronic piano which has six rows of the keyboards, and of which the width of black and white keys is about the same. And one row of keyboard can produce only one note sound. Timbre wise, the top row has the thinnest sound whereas the bottom row has the thickest sound.

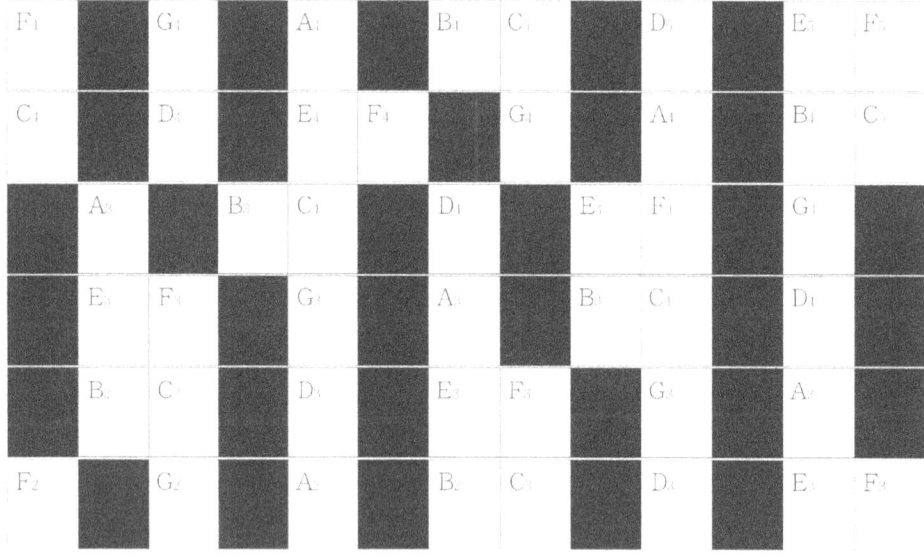

When we use our left hand to play it (imitating your left hand on a guitar to press strings), if you would like to play a melody on a certain row, one single octave then has a very long distance. When opening up your left hand, you may probably only get to play a fifth interval, and the remaining notes then would just be left to left hand to play with a big jump?

For a bunch of melodic lines, the intervals between notes are more than an octave, so then how do you play it nicely, fluently without too much of the hard works? At this time, you then will use keyboards of other rows, musical notes with a fourth interval would be placed in aside; whereas musical notes with an 8th interval would be placed in a lower low. Under a condition where a total of six rows of keyboard can be used to play to an interval of 16th and up without having your hand to do a big jump, is this more convenient for you? And when playing chords, as one row of keyboard can only produce one sound, we therefore need other rows of keyboards to play music. This is why we must know what other individual musical notes are available when keyboards of other rows are on the same position; and when your hand is placed on different key positions, the playable musical notes on six rows of keyboards can be different. This is the so-called different "fret position" concept.

☆ **Then how do we know for the same melody at which fret position should we be playing? And how do we choose ?**

Simply say, there are 3 types of option:

1. Timbre

As mentioned above that timbre of each key is to be quite different (that is to say different strings have different thickness and thinness). Therefore taking one note as an example, if playing one string produces a sound which is too thick or too thin. Or upon connections of melodies, changes of timbre to be quite dramatic and thus aurally we feel it's too sudden, then we will do switching of different fret positions for allowing the melodies to sound more beautiful.

2. Fingering

This then is the question for playing the melodies to be at ease or not, even the starting note of the same melody uses the same position, however, for one time it is to use your index finger to press (on strings) and another time is to use your pinky to press (on strings). Also for the convenience of left hand to play fluently, we would also choose different fret positions to play.

3. Techniques of Musical Expressions

There is quite a big difference between a guitar and a keyboard such as the musical expressions. One expressional technique which has positional changes is glissando. If you would like to have the effects of glissando in one melody, even it is done just with a distance of a whole note, it can let your entire hand to slide to another position. And certainly, for the purpose of a convenient playing, you would need to use the musical notes on particular fret positions to play.

So isn't the memorization and application of musical notes on a fretboard very important?

Chapter FIVE

Building Blocks Moved to Fretboard

So are you now already very fluent in scale building blocks so you can draw them backward? Then next let's start moving them to a fretboard and proceed practices.

♦Individual Practices on the Fretboard

It allows you to be more familiar with the positions and distances of vertical direction musical notes on the same fret position.

1. To play from the lowest note to the highest note, while playing along and reading out the solfege of musical notes. On the contrary, playing from the highest note to the lowest note and repeat the same practices.

Pitch name	C	D	E	F	G	A	B
Solfege	Do	Re	Mi	Fa	Sol	La	Si
Numbered musical notation	1	2	3	4	5	6	7

* Codes for left hand fingers: 1-Index finger 2-Middle finger 3-Ring finger 4-Pinky

The 3rd fret building block

[Track-1]

The 5th fret building block

[Track-2]

The 7th fret building block

[Track-3]

The 10th fret building block

[Track-4]

THE PRACTICE : And, Strengthen Your Memories

The 12th fret building block (this is of the same style to an open note)

[Track-5]

2. Please pay attention to the fretboard position where each building block locates, using finger position marks to help your memory (finger position marks often appear at the 3rd, 5th, 7th and 9th frets.)

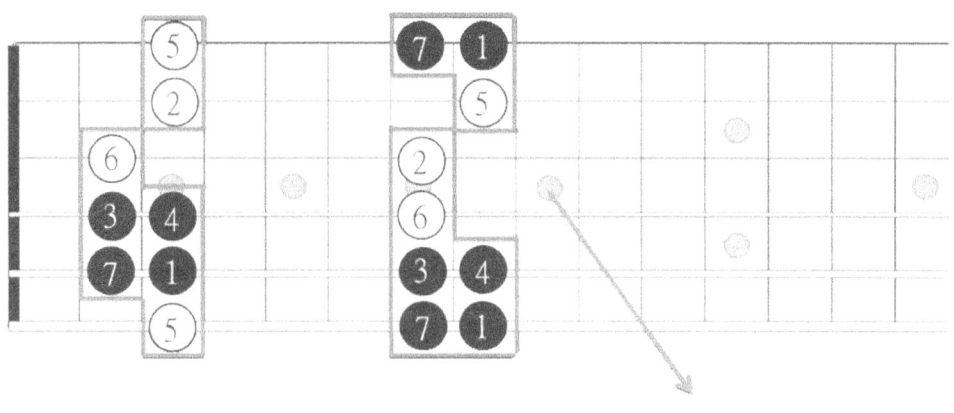

Position mark

3. Randomly jumping around and practicing building block graphic of different positions. You may ask a friend to test you randomly, for instance, when he says "the 5th fret", you then must play the building block on the 5th fret and then say the solfege name or the pitch name of each musical note. And then please have him or her verify your answer to be correct or not.

4. If the above mentioned approaches seem very familiar to you, and they has been correct without any mistake, then you can enter advanced versions of training: directly point at a position at any place and then say what musical note it is. It is like the practice below.

◆Quiz

Please name the solfege name and pitch name for the musical notes below. (A kind reminder for you, please manage yourself not to start counting from an open note.)

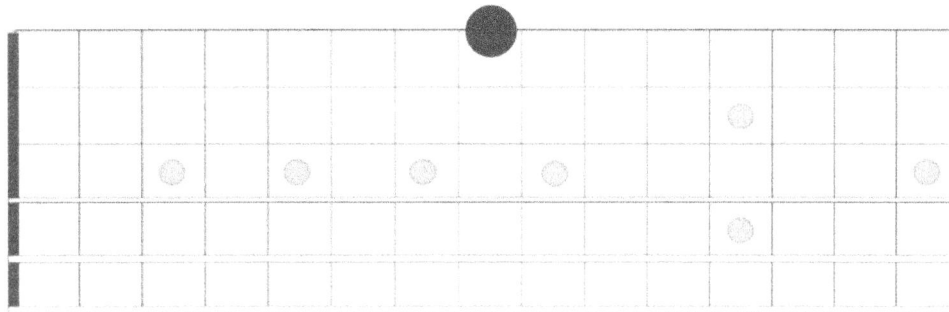

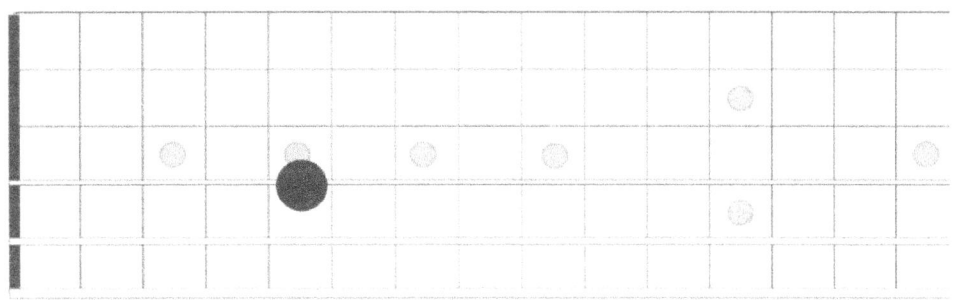

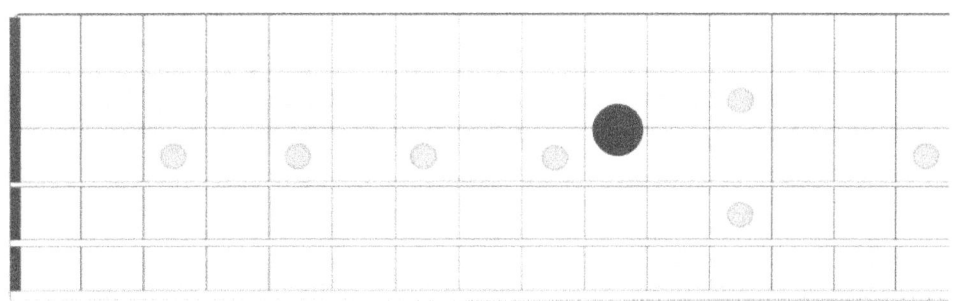

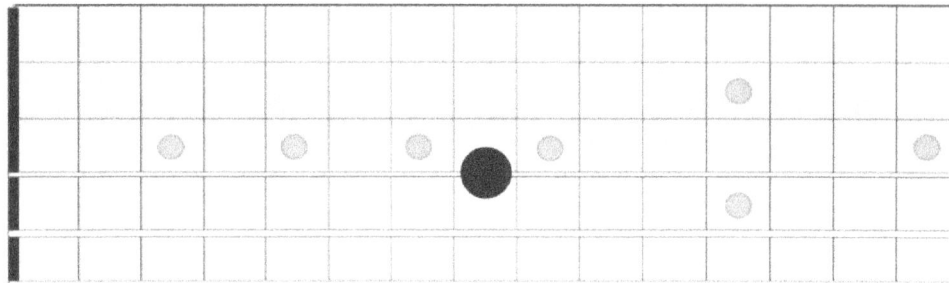

This is the most commonly seen 5 pattern practice. Likewise, it is like playing from the lowest note to the highest note, and from the highest note to the lowest note. While playing along and singing out the solfege of musical notes, and thinking about how the 2 building block graphics are like on the fretboard.

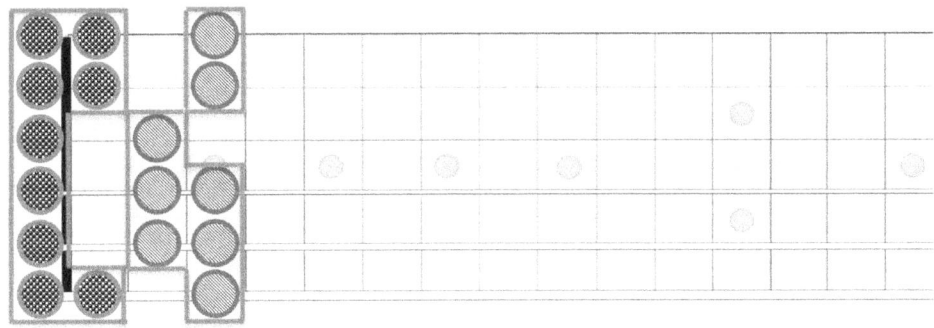

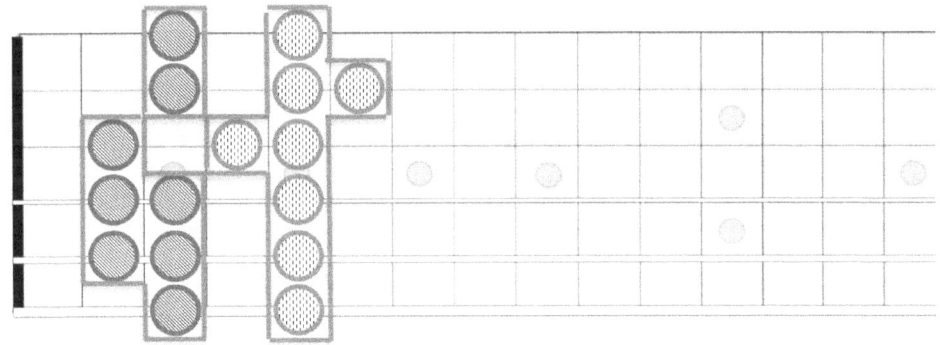

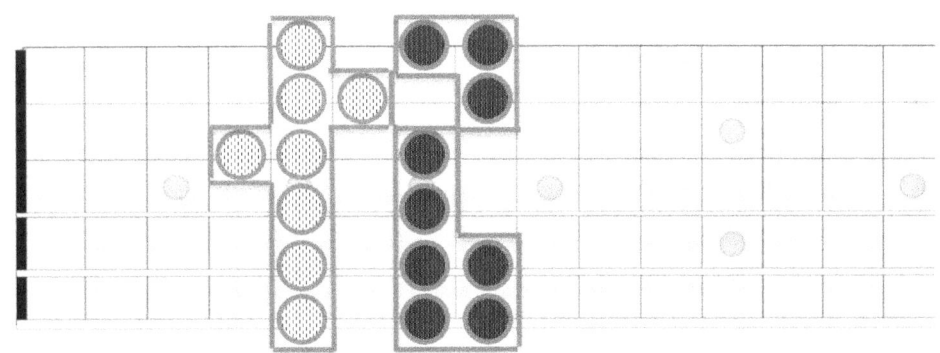

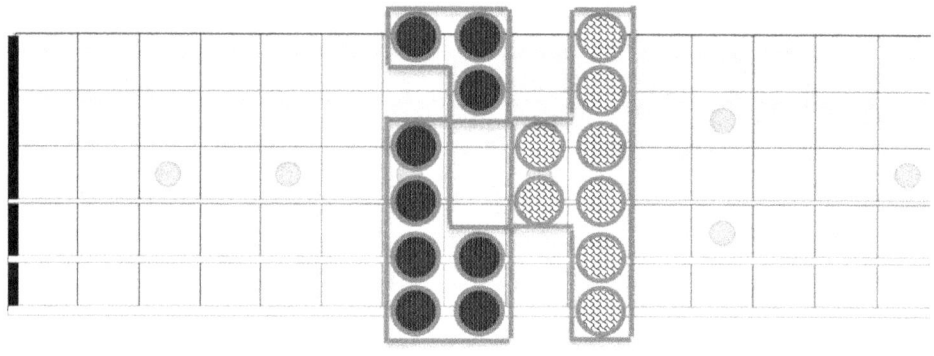

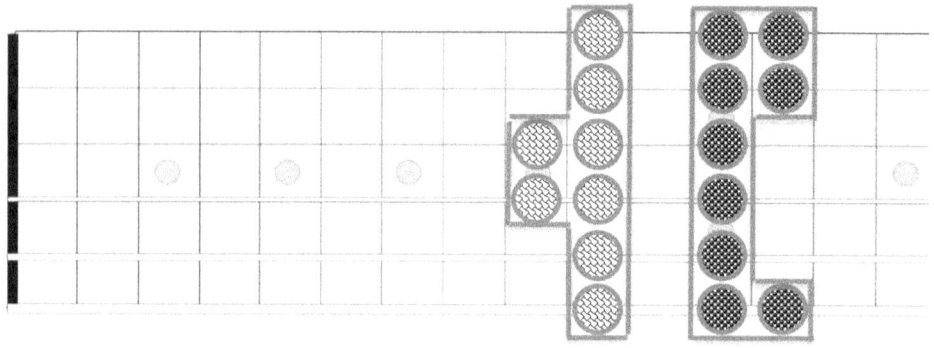

Example: Pattern 2 practice method:

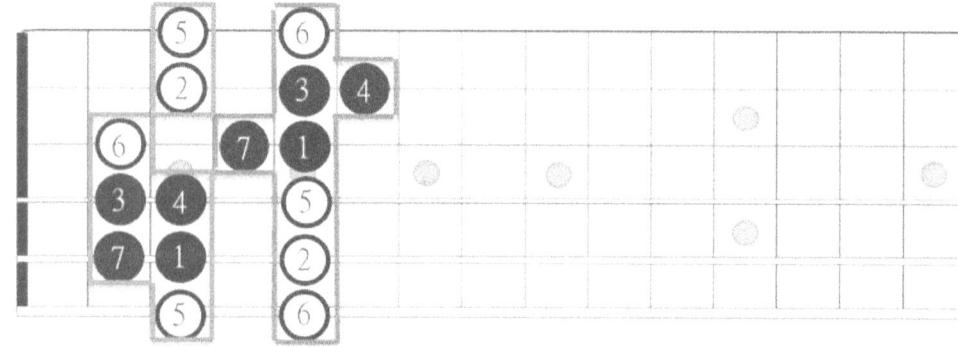

(1)

[Track-6]

(2)

[Track-7]

6

11

(3)

[Track-8]

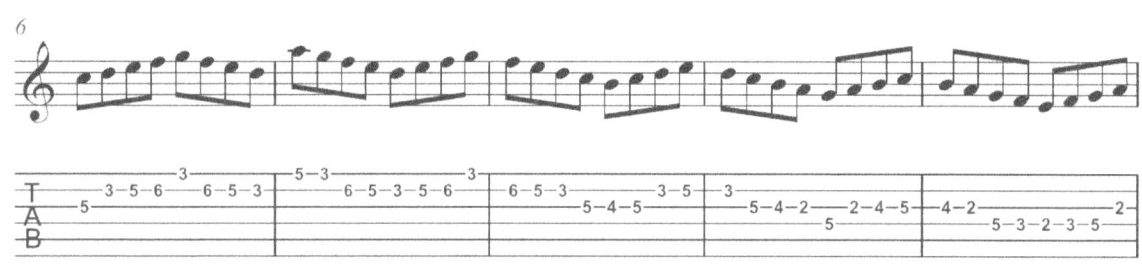

This is a practice which allows you to strum chords while playing fill-ins as your goal.

1. First please strum a chord, like C.

2. Move your hands to chord roots of different fret positions and then play scales in a descending or an ascending direction.

3. And then please strum the second chord, such as Am and repeat the 2nd step.

4. Use chord progression approach to continue such practice. While playing a single note scale, you may be able to choose a different fret position.

Example:

(Pattern 4)

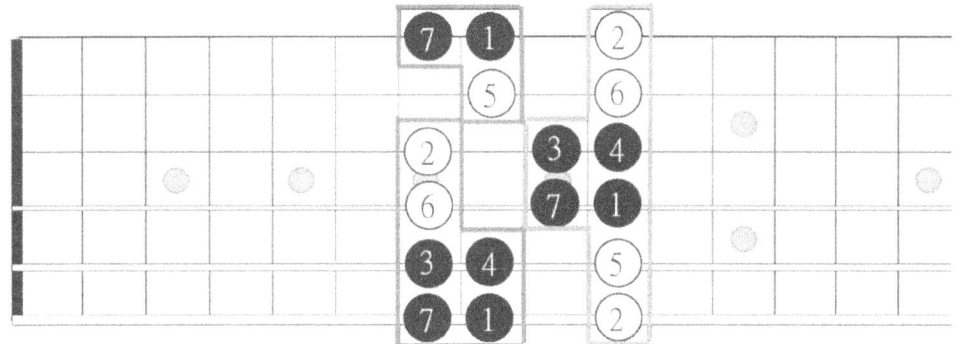

[Track-9]

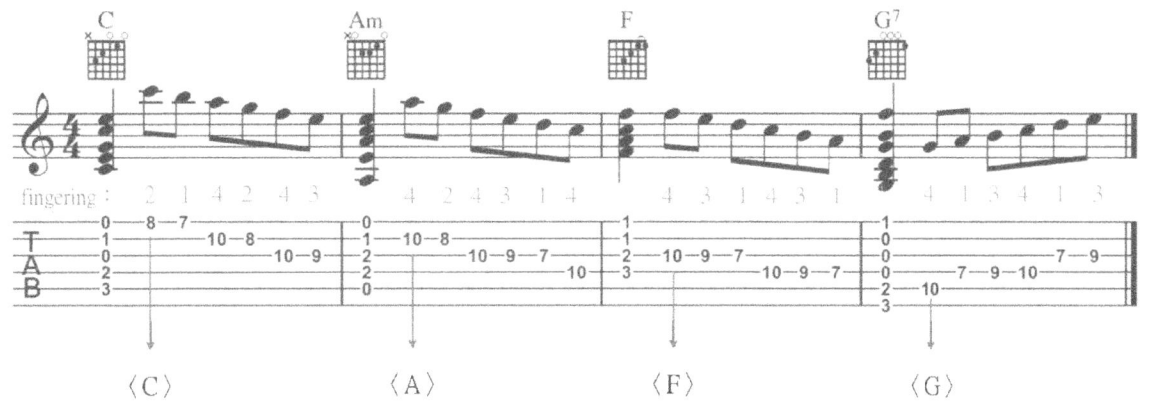

(Pattern 3)

[Track-10]

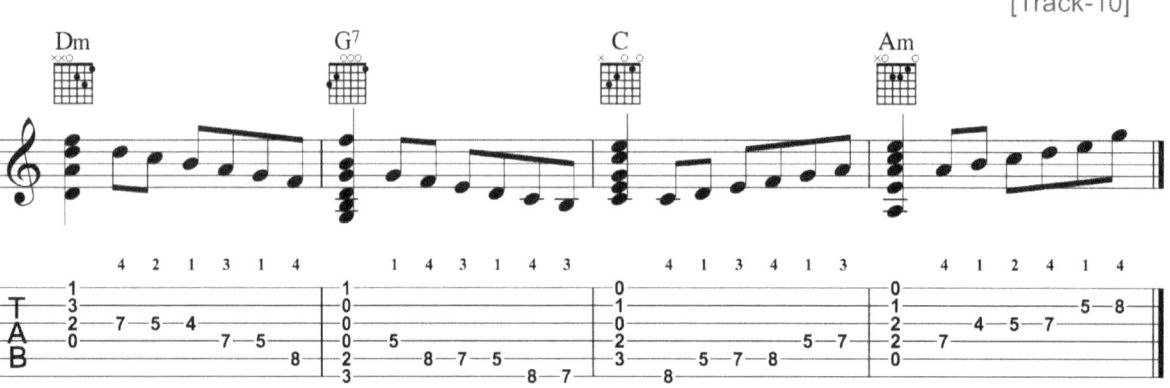

5. Then, random the scale notes and patterns.

[Track-11]

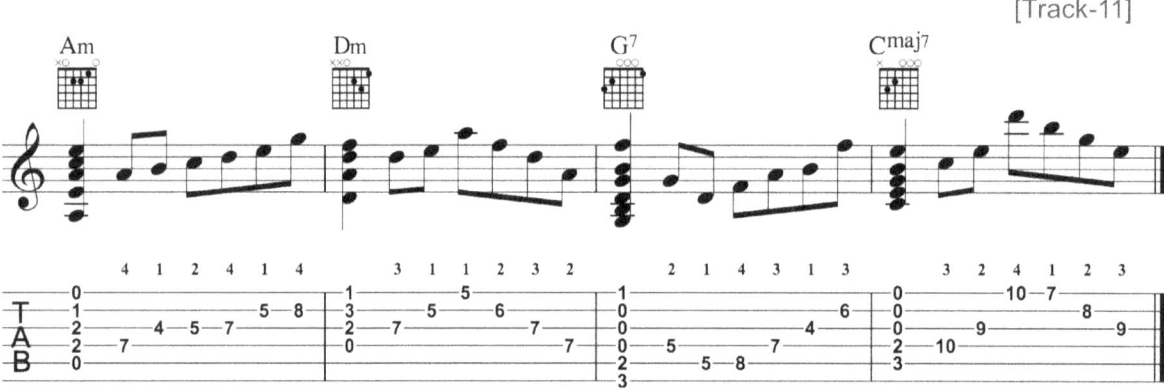

■ Bar 1 ~ Bar 3 : Pattern 3,

■ Bar 4 : Pattern 4

Section 4 Playing the same melody on different fret positions

Taking the melody of "Twinkle Twinkle Little Star" as one example, its numbered musical notation is:

| 1155 | 665- | 4433 | 221- |

| 5544 | 332- | 5544 | 332- |

| 1155 | 665- | 4433 | 221- |

We can play this melody individually in the pattern fret positions below:

(1) This pattern has 2 sets for you to play.

(Play1) [Track-12]

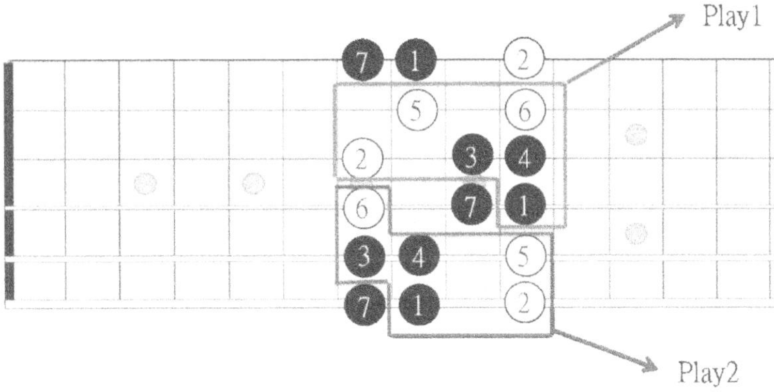

(Play2) [Track-13]

(2) This pattern also has 2 sets for you to play, and you can try to find it on your own.

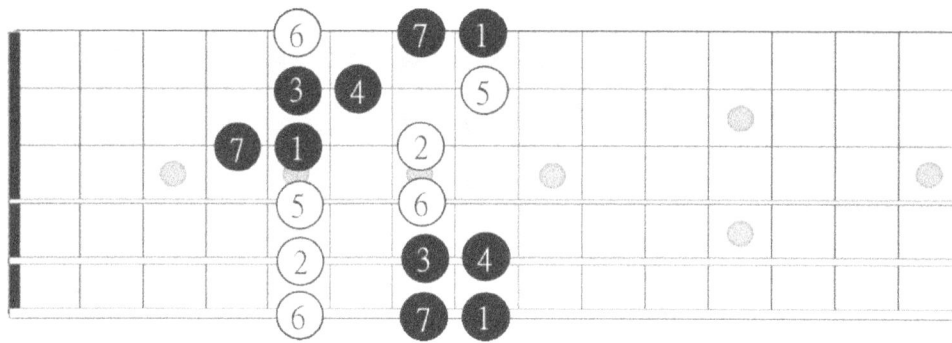

(3) There are also 2 sets for this pattern to play.

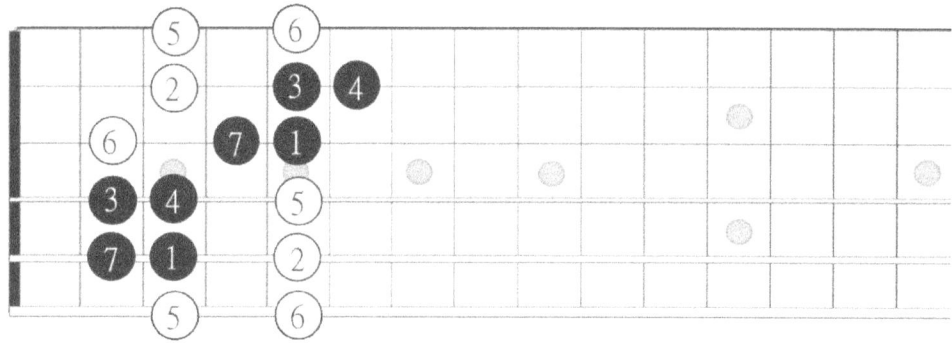

(4) This pattern also has 1 set for you to play.

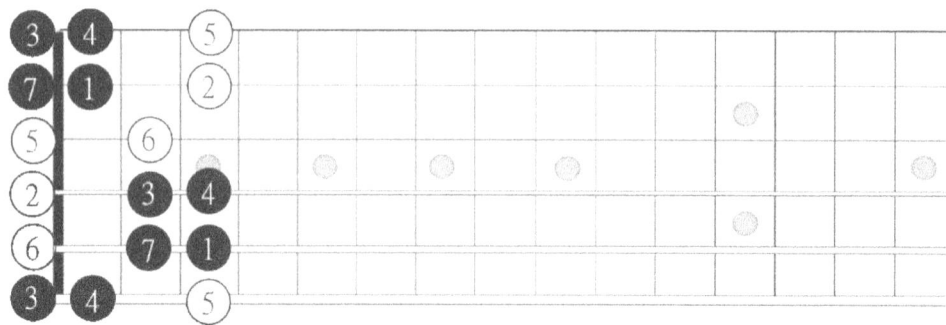

Next we can continue to use other simple songs, such as the 'Lightly Row' and 'Ode to Joy', or you may open up other popular music method books for playing songs in numbered musical notation to practice.

Chapter SIX

Horizontal Shift of Building Blocks

The fingering graphics we use previously belong to no sharps and no flats C Major scale format graphic. However, it is just that not every piece of music is in C key. So what do we do when the music is in other keys? On a guitar, all you need to do is to move the scale building block graphics horizontally.

This is so called "transposition." This is also a very good practice for you being familiar with the fretboard and building block graphics.

♦Horizontal Moving Practices

1. <u>First please move C Major building block graphic horizontally</u>

Assuming the music we would like to play is in G major then let's take tonic 1 position and move it horizontally to G note. This way, the shown building block graphics are then a G Major graphic.

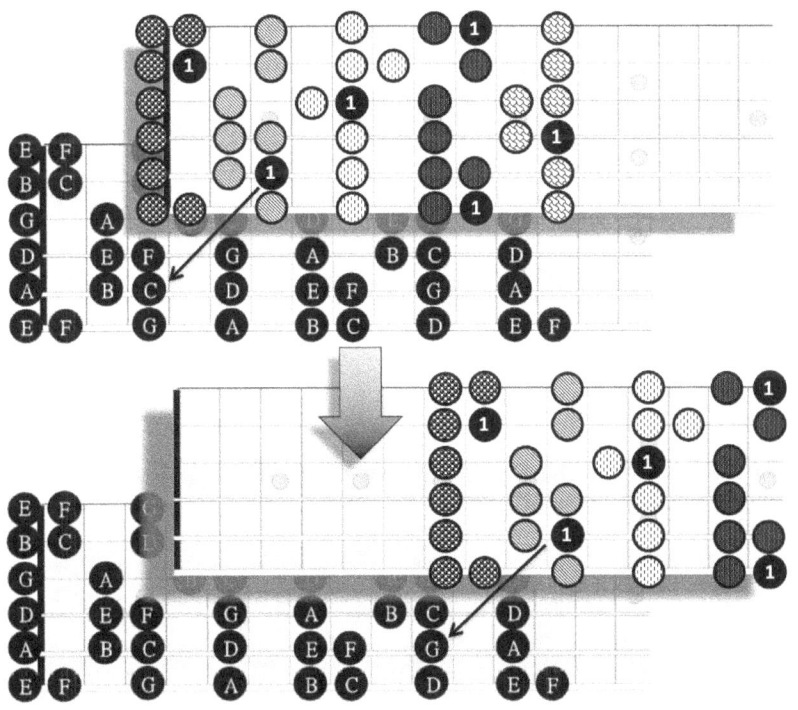

2. <u>To make up to the necessary circulation of scale building block graphic in the previous section</u>

There are certainly musical notes available in the previous blank spaces, you can simply follow the building block circulation graphics and make it up.

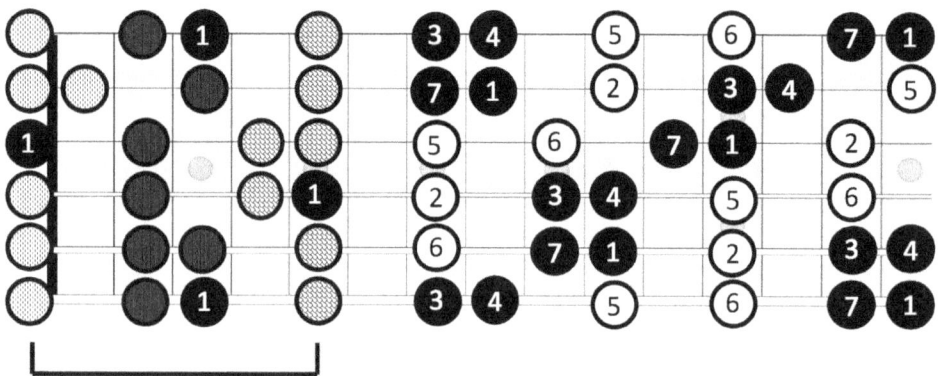

3. <u>Practices on the Fretboard</u>

Follow the practice order in the previous chapter to practice and see what happens. Actually the graphics remain unchanged and it is just the positions that change. After many practices you then can get used to such circulation changes on the graphics.

4. <u>Other Major Key Scale Practices</u>

You may start practicing from keys which you often see, such as the keys of A, D and E. These are also considered as the often-used keys. After you have slightly practiced more keys, you then will discover the circulation building block graphics to be much easier to present!

< E Key >

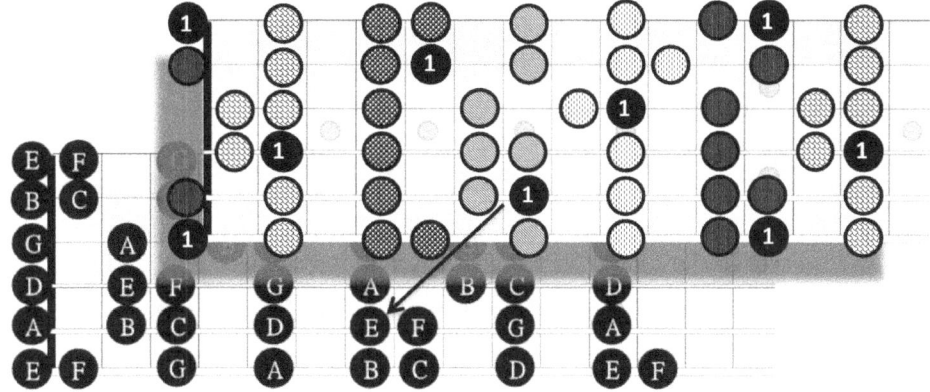

< A Key >

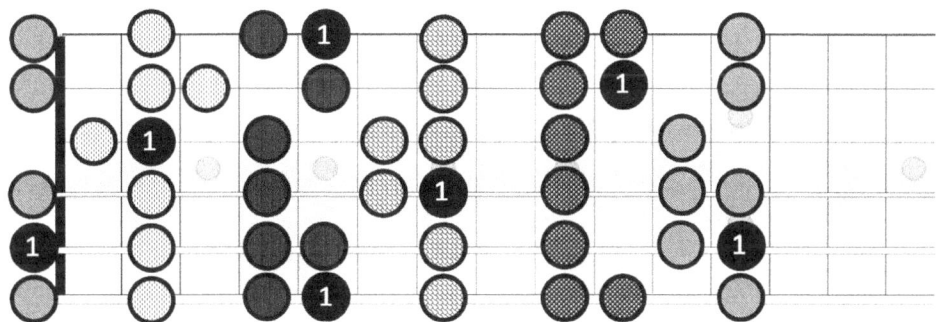

< D Key >

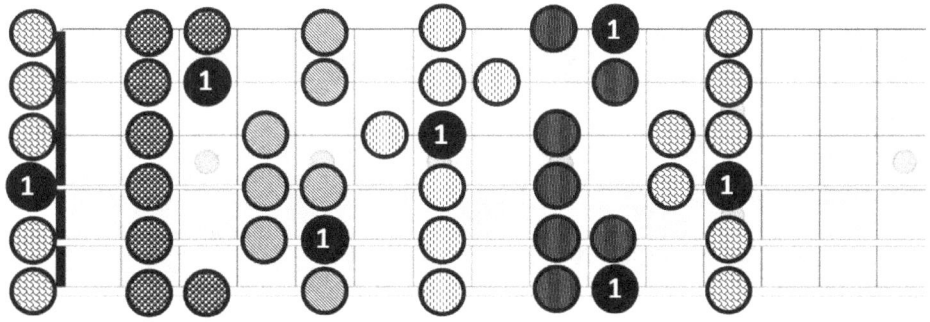

♦ Explanations for Small Questions

☆ **For transpositions, is it doable to simply move the graphics horizontally to different frets, without changing the numbers ?**

Firstly let's explain the numbers. Numbers refers to numbered musical notations and one certain number is a note in a major key scale, 1 as the 1st note, 2 as the 2nd note and so on. For instance, 1 in C key represents the note C; however, if it's in G key, it represents the note G. Musical notes are like the reference chart below:

	1	2	3	4	5	6	7
C Key	C	D	E	F	G	A	B
G Key	G	A	B	C	D	E	F#

This way, you can also discover why it can be done by simply moving the graphics horizontally, is that right? You may directly try to circle a building block graphic of G key scale on a diatonic scale graphic then you will know the answers.

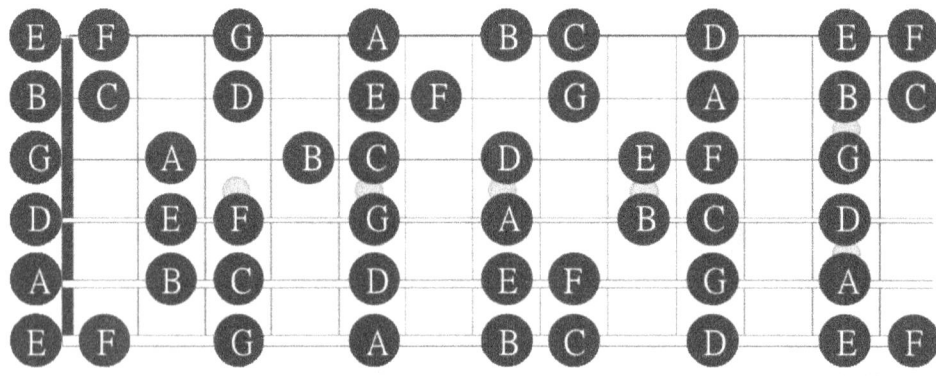

After the previous practices have allowed us to be more familiar with the changes of graphics as well as number scales, next we would like to practice the relations between graphics and pitch names well after transpositions.

For examples, graphics of G key are formed by using the position of 1 aiming at G note and move horizontally. Therefore, we get to know the position of 1 is G note. However this is not enough. We need to learn to know that in this graphic, 2 is A note, 3 is B note, 4 is C note...., we need to know all the exact pitch names at all positions.

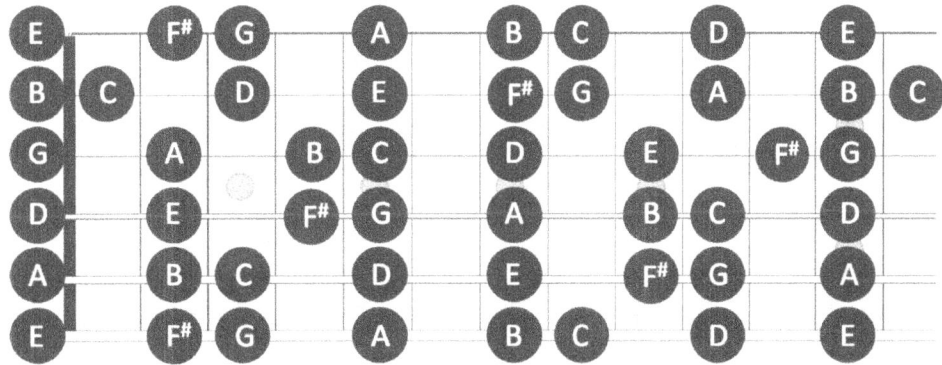

As the building block graphic is an efficient assisting tool, however, essentially, we need to learn the followings through it:

1. Positions of solmization (pitch names)
2. In each key, the relative distances between musical notes (that is every type of interval).

One song may encounter continuous key modulations upon playing or using different scales. If at this time, you are too rigidly adhere to moving the graphics, you may make the playing too complicated. This is like playing Jazz Blues styles music where G note may be the 1st note in G key in the beginning but it quickly modulates to a different key on the next beat. Or it appears in the melodies of chromatic or diminished scales, and at this time, what graphics or numbers would you use to respond to it or to comprehend it?

Actually at this time, we may simply follow the distributions of musical notes in a natural scale to play music and that is it. Whenever it is, a G note is a G note. In additional to knowing it is a G, moreover, you can rely on your hearing to feel what feelings G expresses in background music. And this is true for each musical note or scale until the end.

Therefore, the most important matter for building block graphic practices is the handling of pitch name positions in a natural scale on a guitar.

And, why is musical interval also important?

This is because aurally, two notes with the same interval have the same distance. And because of the design of fret on the guitar, the relative position is said to be the same. For instance, taking a major 3rd interval as an example, C and E which move toward higher notes, and A and C$^{\#}$ which move toward higher notes, have the same interval as well as the same relative positions on the guitar. This is shown below:

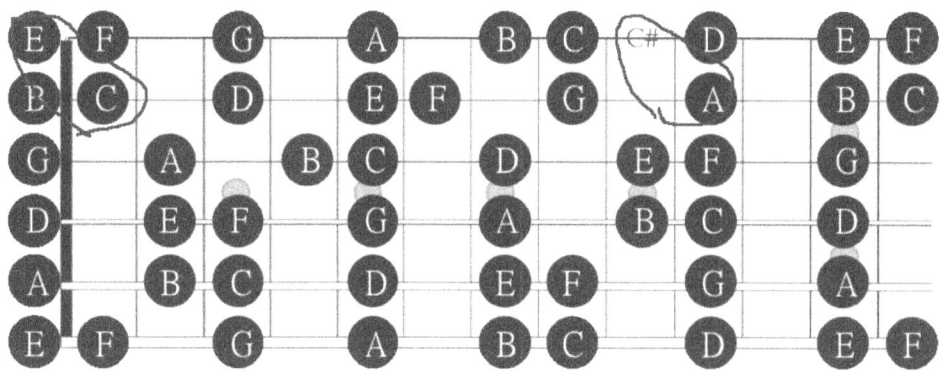

Musically when we hear our own melody plays to a C note, and we would like to add a major 3rd pitch in the back, then your fingers which are familiar with the relative positions can directly respond and play to E note position. Similarly, when we play an A note and then we discover the key will modulate to A key, and in the same time, you would like to play a major 3rd interval C$^{\#}$ which matches the key, your fingers then can just go ahead and directly press on a major 3rd interval position. By doing so, you can follow your heart to play the guitar, isn't that just wonderful?

This then is the practice of building block graphic horizontal movement along with keys for helping everyone to achieve his goals. Upon practices, please bear in mind that you will need to remember these goals and concepts so that the image memorization method can actually show its power.

Chapter SEVEN

Building Blocks which Combine Other Graphics

For the purpose of convenient memorization, each string in "One String Three Notes" circulation graphic has a setup of a perfect fourth interval tuning string among each other; therefore, when touching the 2nd string and 3rd string to cross over, you must move one fret to meet the real fingering; however, the building block graphic can be used without any modification. There are advantages and disadvantages for both graphics, and there's a complementary function in applications, therefore after you are familiar with them individually and combine both together, it will be even more efficient for you to be familiar with the fretboard!

Application wise, the graphic of "One String Three Notes" is more suitable for collaborating an ascending melodic performance whereas the building block graphic is more suitable for string crossing-over or every type of arpeggio performance. Being familiar with both is like the getting through the 'governor and conception vessels' in a "guitar chi-exercise" (Note: based on traditional Chinese medicine theory, the governor and conception vessels are the two important vessels in a human body for mastering Chinese martial arts.)

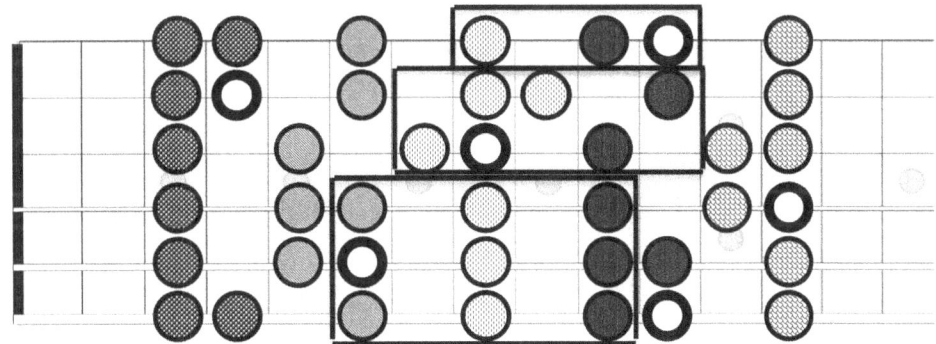

◆Quiz

Please frame what building block graphics do the following graphics belong to, and make up the incomplete building block graphics.

<1>

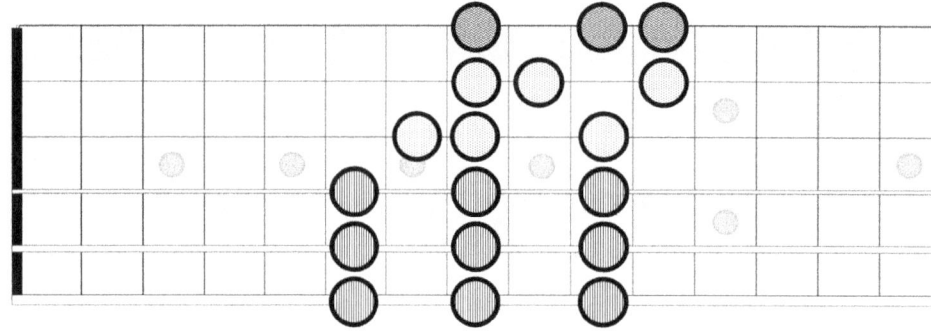

<2>

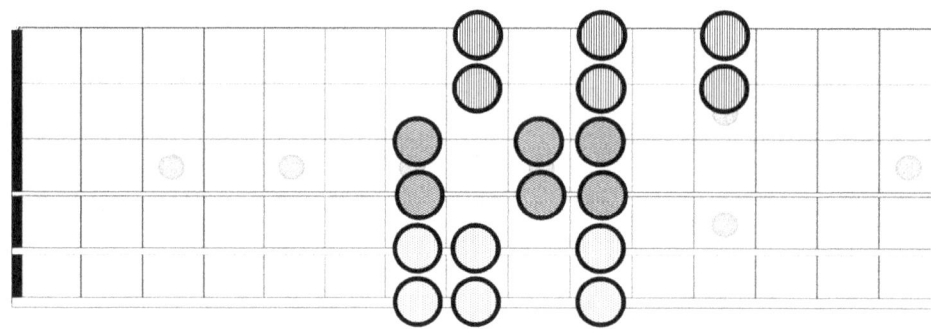

<3>

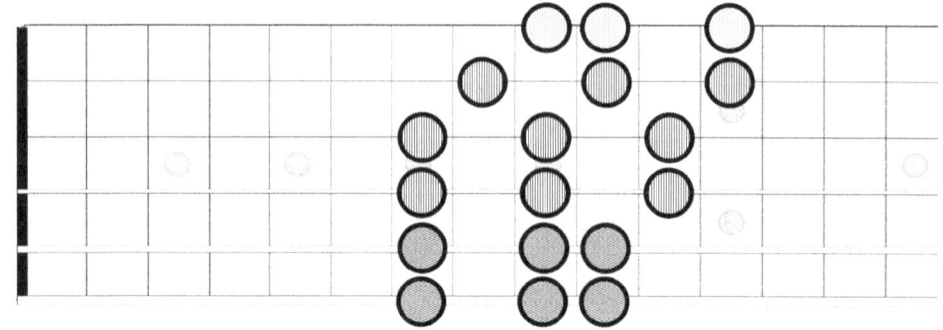

◆Examples after getting through the governor and conception vessels

<1>

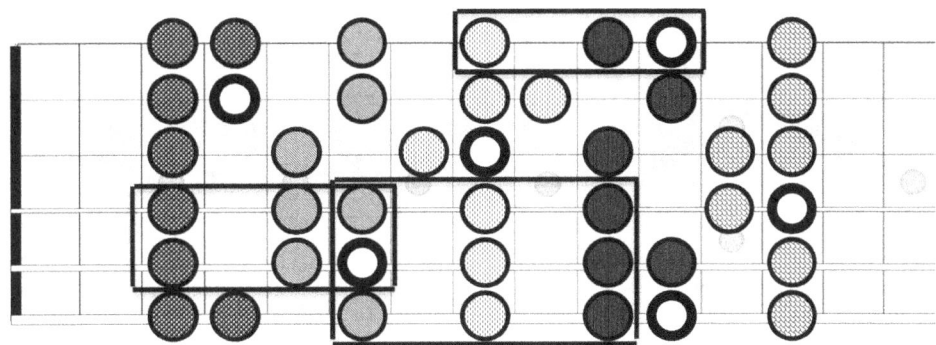

In this example, the below circulation graphic fingering uses glissando(slide) as a connection and in the middle section, an arpeggio form is used to connect to the above 3 notes on the 1st string. And then an arpeggio form is used again to return to the below circulation graphic fingering. In the end, glissando ends at another circulation graphic fingering.

[Track-14]

fingering : 1 2 4 2 4 2 2 1   2 3 4 3   2 3   1 4 1 3 4 3 2 3   2 1   3 4

<2>

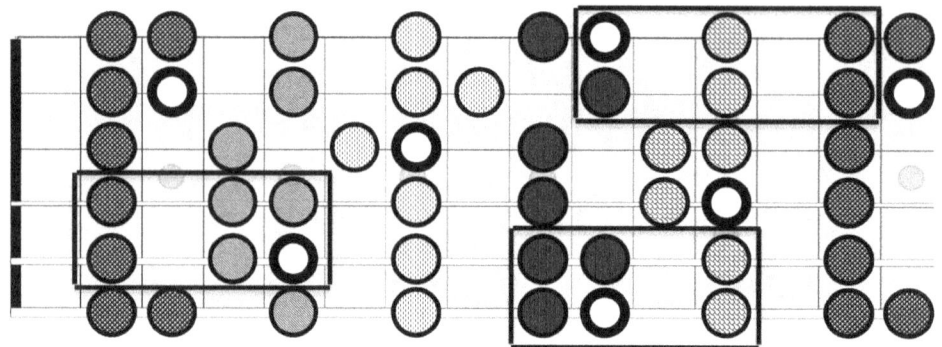

This example starts from the bass note of the 10th fret on the 6th string in a higher fret position. An arpeggio form is used to play up to the 12th fret of the 1st string and then an arpeggio is used to play downward to return to the recent circulation graphic fingering. In the end, glissando reaches the 4th fret of the 4th string in a low fret position and ends at a D note.

[Track-15]

1. Adding jumping musical notes of one octave interval when playing the melodies

<1>

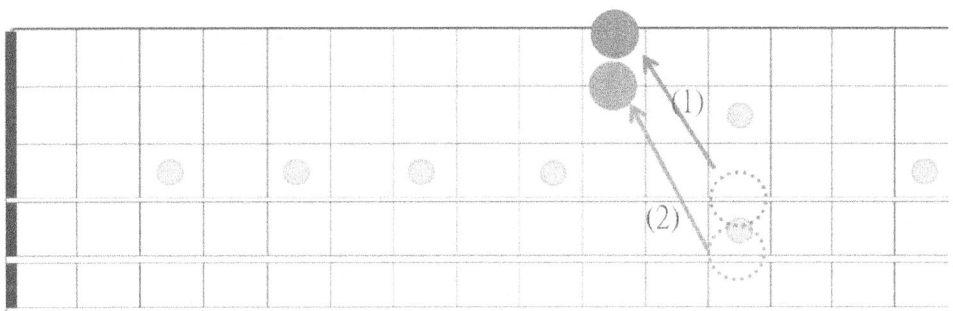

[Track-16]

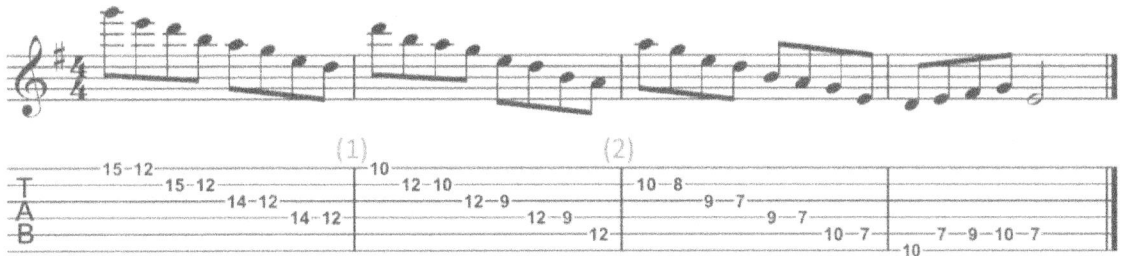

fingering : 4 1 4 1 3 1 3 2   1 3 1 4 1 4 1 4   2 1 3 1 3 1 4 1   4 1 3 4 1

<2>

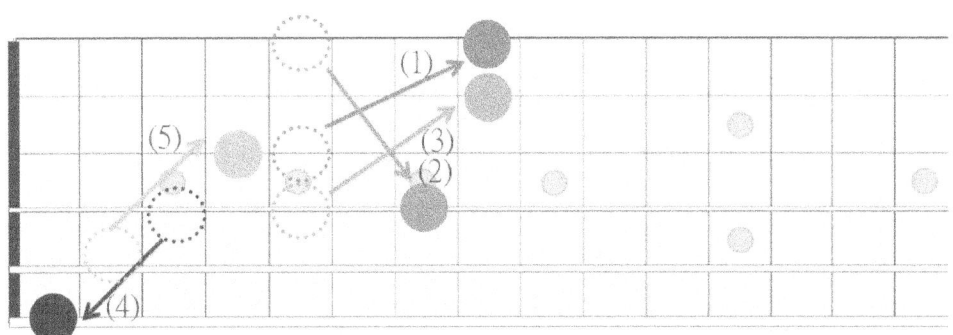

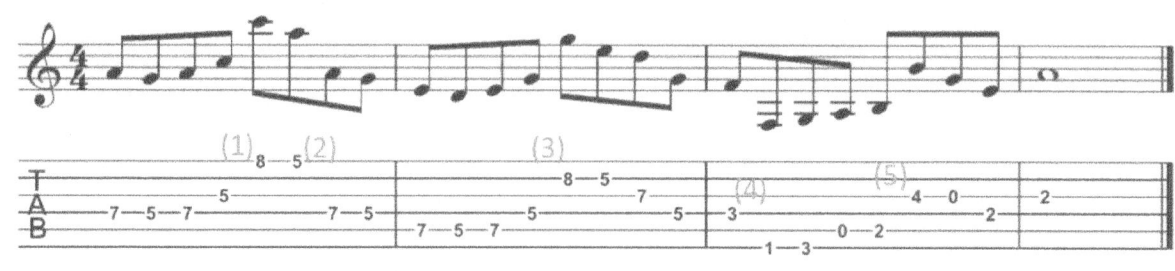

2. Using an octave to jump to another fret position to play

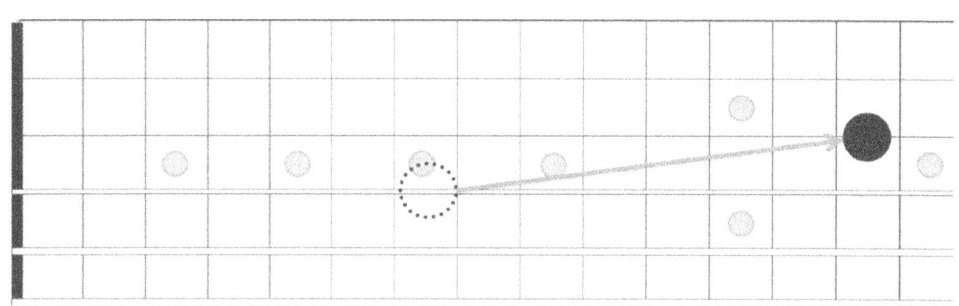

[Track-18]

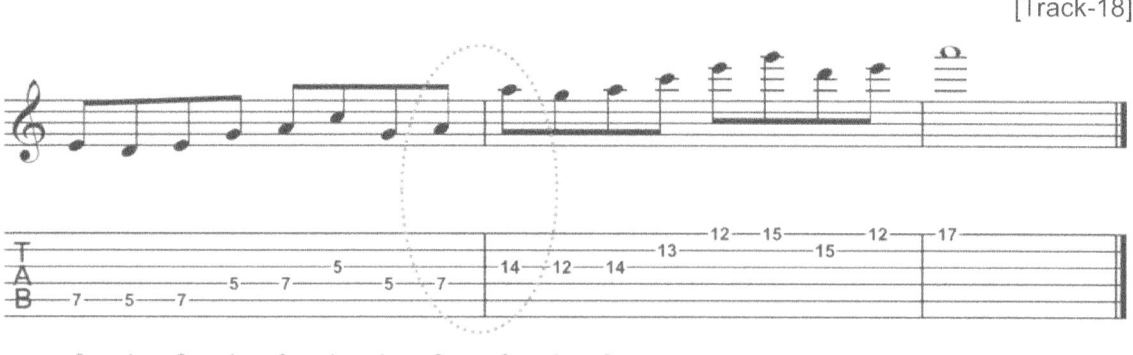

Chapter EIGHT

Uses of Interval and Double-Stop

Previously, it has mentioned that we want to use a building block graphic to learn about relative positions of interval, regardless of improvisation or the emotional handling and applications represented by interval, it is quite important. Next, we will use double stop to practice handling aural effects of interval and interval positions on a fretboard.

♦Perfect Fifth & Perfect Fourth

Taking scales as an example, 1st note and 5th note have a relation of a perfect fifth and 1st and 4th have a perfect fourth relation. Therefore, their relative positions on the fretboard are:

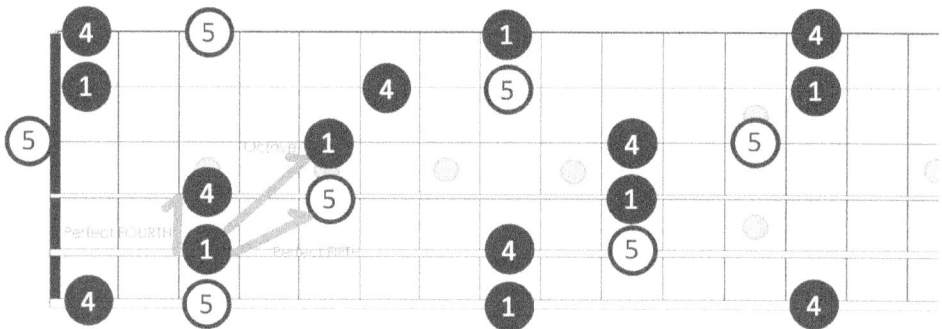

If we put the 5th note and the octave 1st note together to view, hasn't their interval then become a perfect fourth?

In addition to 1-5 notes in the scale, by following the scale moving up in an ascending direction, 2-6, 3-7, 4-1, 5-2 and 6-3 all have the same interval relation, only 7-4 will be a diminished fifth, and 4-7 is an augmented fourth which has the same distance as a diminished fifth.

■ In Rock n' roll music, the double-stop of fifth and fourth intervals often use a 'Power Chord' to present.

■ There are 2 ways to find a perfect fifth of a musical note on a fretboard:

(a) When an index finger presses on that certain musical note

(b) When it's not an index finger pressing on that certain musical note

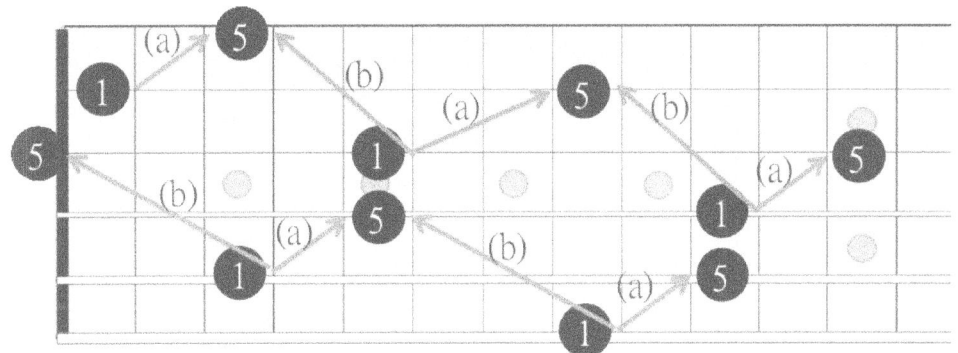

<1>

[Track-19]

fingering :   3
             1

<2>

[Track-20]

In addition to the 2nd and 3rd strings, an interval of fourth is right on a neighboring string located on the same fret.

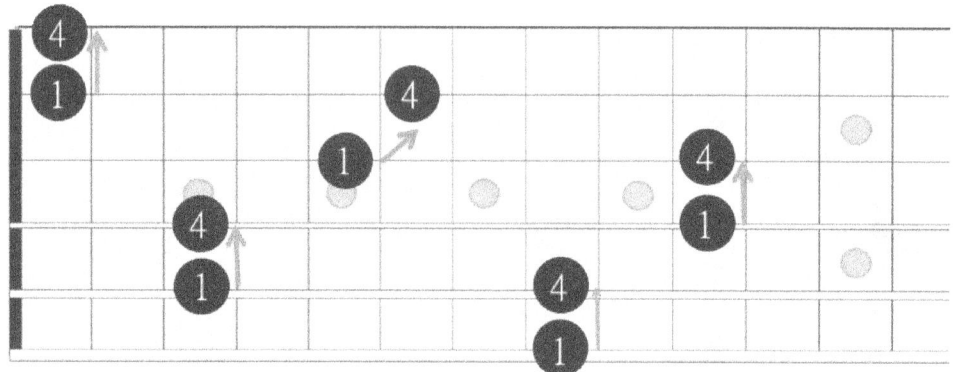

<1>

[Track-21]

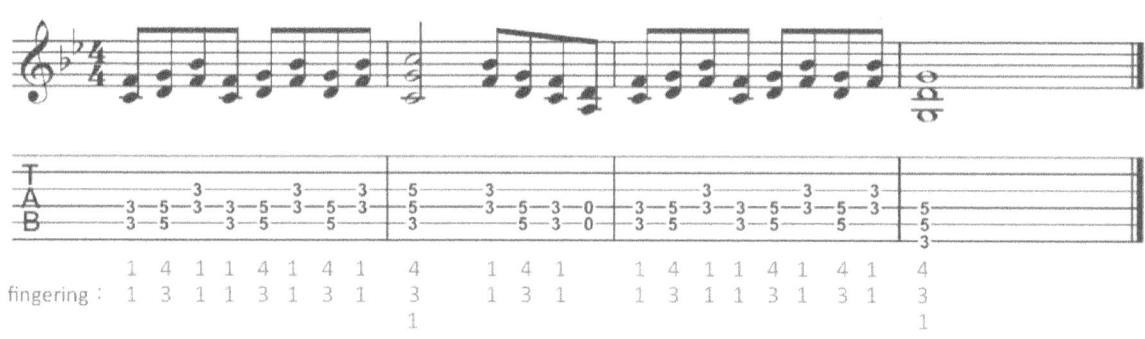

<2>

[Track-22]

★ Attention please: if it has crossed to the 2nd string, there will be a change of 1 fret.

Taking scales as one example, 1st note and 3rd note have a relation of a major third, therefore, 1st note and ᵇ3 note is a minor third. Their relative positions on a fretboard are as below:

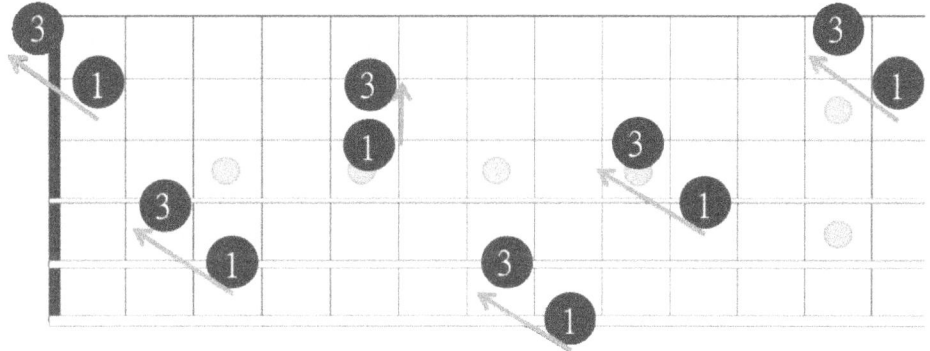

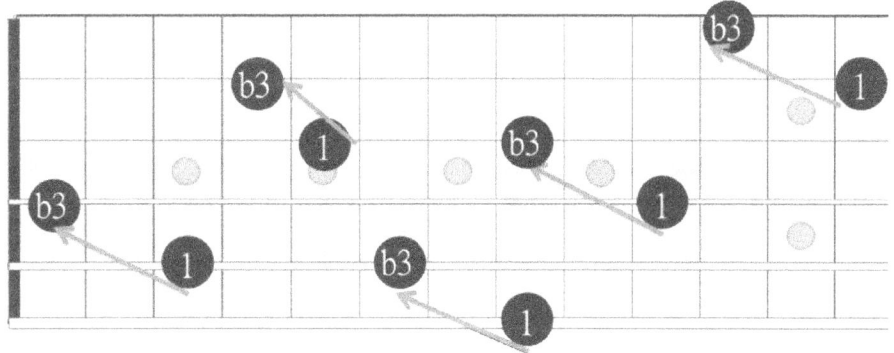

■ A distance of a third interval is very suitable for double-stop performance and this is because a chord is comprised of musical notes which are piling up with a third interval. When we follow a scale in an ascending direction to play a third interval double-stop, its format actually will be:

1 - 3 Major Third

2 - 4 Minor Third

3 - 5 Minor Third

4 - 6 Major Third

5 - 7 Major Third

6 - 1 Minor Third

7 - 2 Minor Third

Therefore when we play melodic lines of a third interval double stop, you may approximately follow this format for your playing.

<1>

[Track-23]

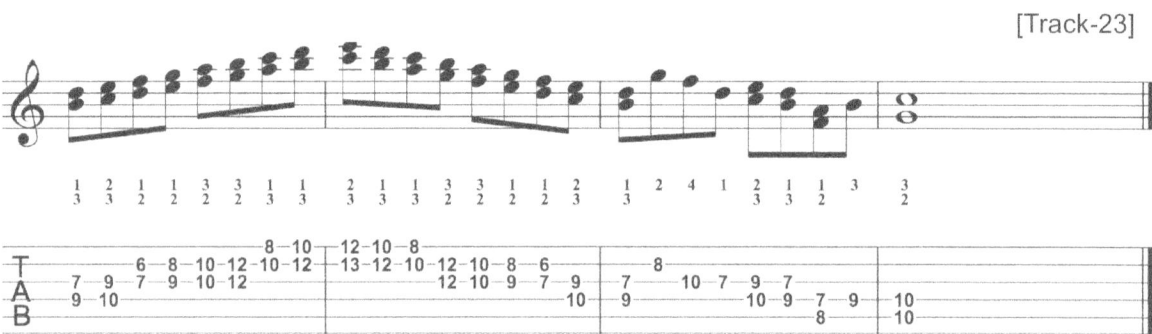

<2>

[Track-24]

■ A distance of a third interval is very suitable for double-stop performance and this is because a chord is comprised of musical notes which are piling up with a third interval. When we follow a scale in an ascending direction to play a third interval double-stop, its format actually will be:

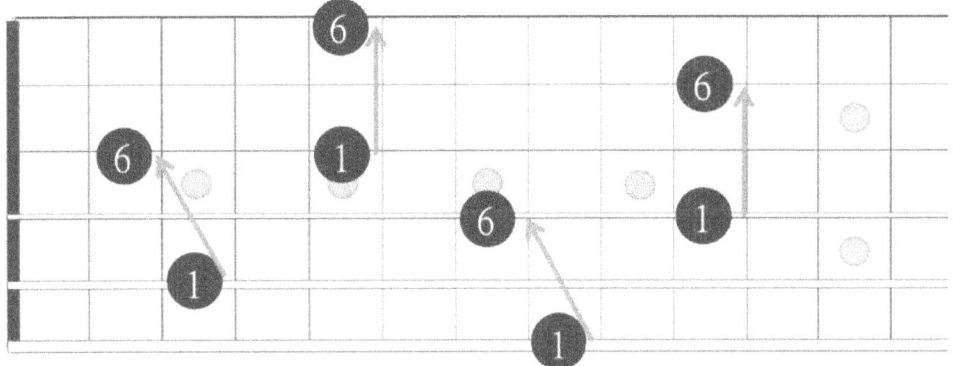

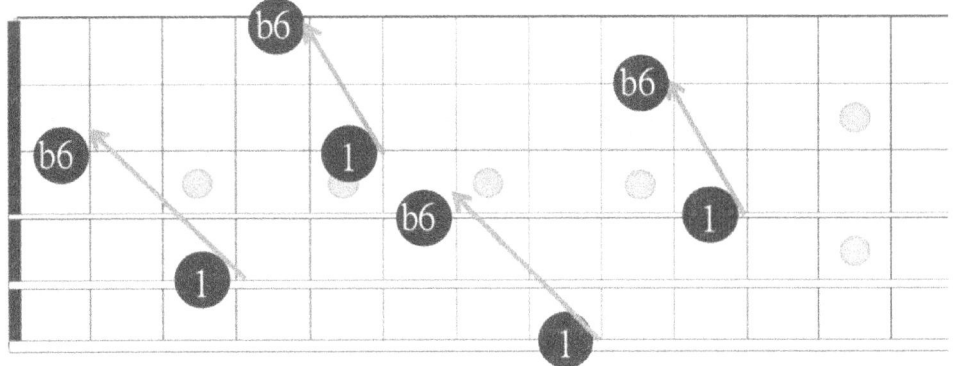

The arrangement of a major and a minor sixth in a scale are as below:

1-6 Major sixth

2-7 Major sixth

3-1 Minor sixth

4-2 Major sixth

5-3 Major sixth

6-4 Minor sixth

7-5 Minor sixth

Therefore, when playing melodic lines of a sixth interval double-stop, you may approximately follow this format for your playing.

<1>

[Track-25]

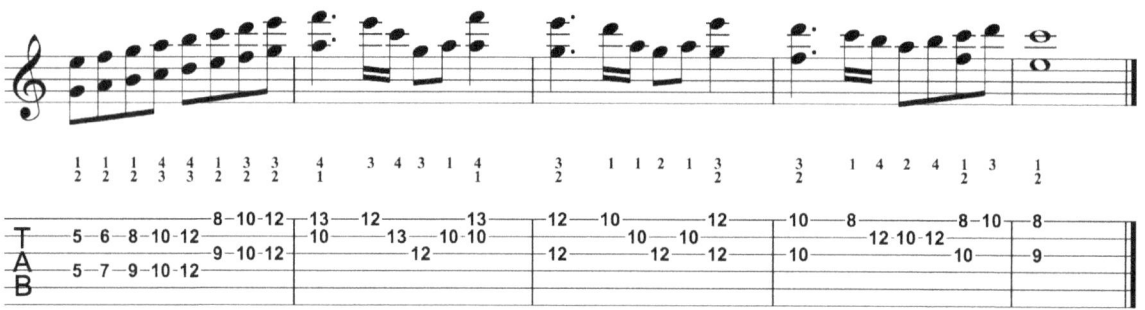

<2>

[Track-26]

■ The playing of octave double-stop is often used in Jazz music. It has more of a taste of smooth Jazz when matching with your right hand thumb plucking strings. For positional relations, please refer to the previous "Position Graphic of Octave".

<1>

[Track-27]

<2>

[Track-28]

THE APPLICATIONS : Final, Enhances Practices Everywhere

■ As musical notes in major and minor seventh among contemporary chords are often used, and also the notes carry special colors and produce dynamics, therefore, being familiar with their positions is also quite important.

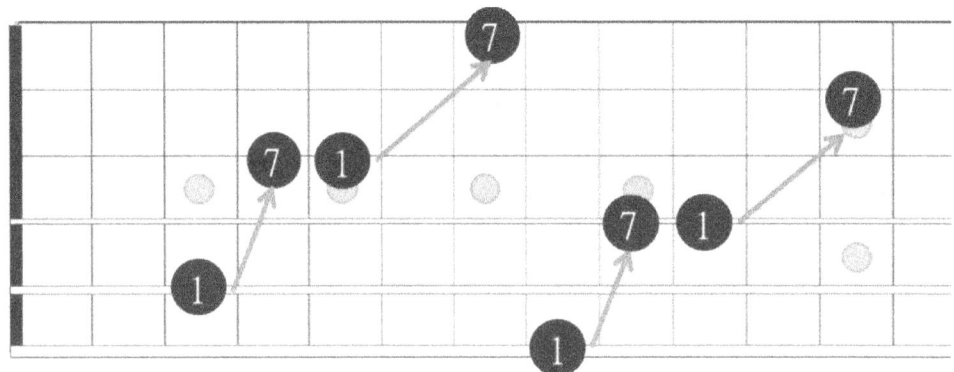

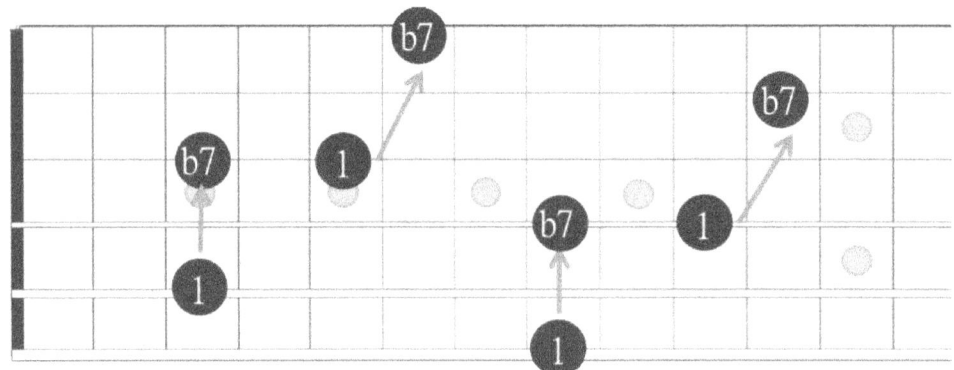

■ When we are able to handle the relations of this interval position, we then can add double-stop in melodic lines more at ease to play. When playing music, we would roughly follow different chord progressions for playing double-stop of different intervals.

Example:

[Track-29]

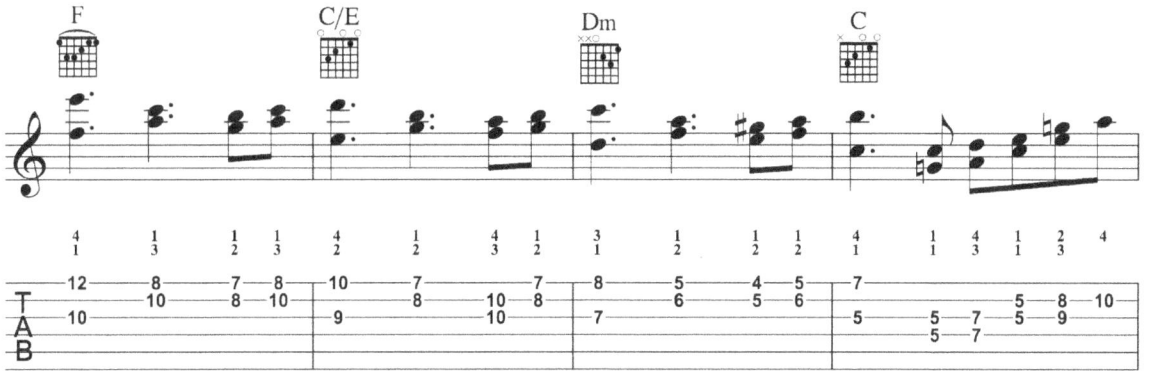

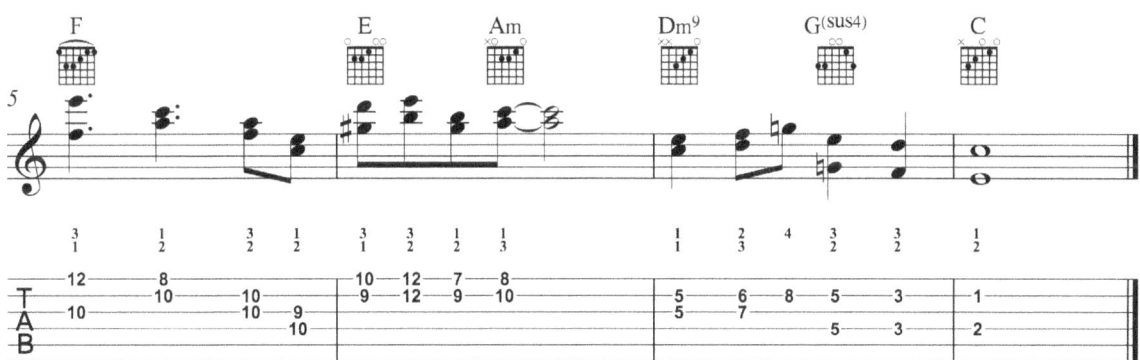

Chapter NINE

Performances of Chord and Fill-Ins

♦Major Third Chord

About the pressing methods of chord on a fretboard, using a basic major third chord as an example, you can follow the pressing methods suitable for your left hand to sum up one chord. There are five basic pressing methods on a fretboard.

(a)   When placing root on the 6th string, you can (1) have your index finger pressing on root, or (2) not using your index finger to press on root. There are two approaches.

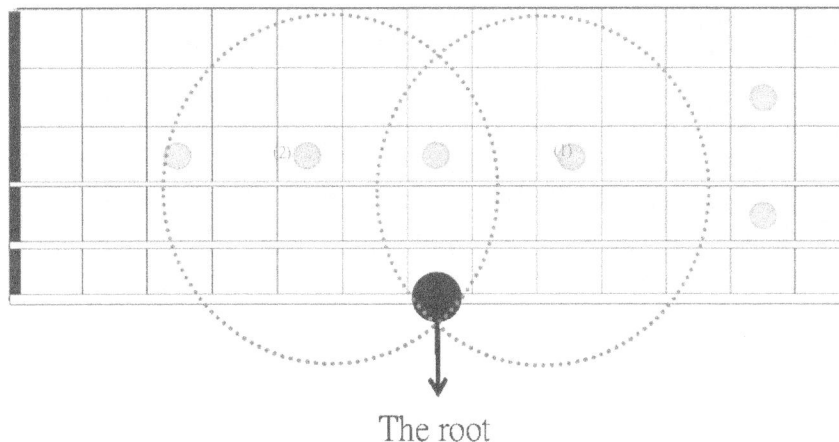

The root

(b)   When placing root on the 5th string, you can (3) have your index finger pressing on root, or (4) not using your index finger to press on root. There are two approaches.

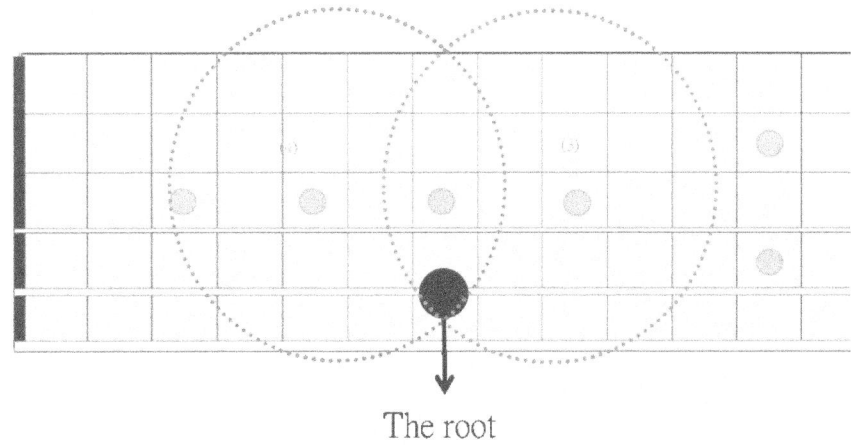

The root

(c)　When placing root on the 4th string, you can (5) have your index finger pressing on root, however (6) the fingering without using your index finger to press root will repeat with (1), therefore, there is only method here.

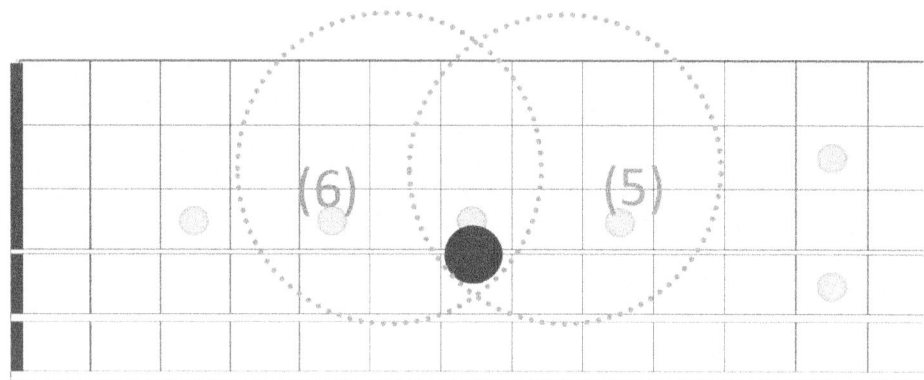

Therefore, the five fingerings of different positions of a major third chord are as below.　If you view this from a higher fret position, you can discover that the graphic circulates continuously:

C Chord

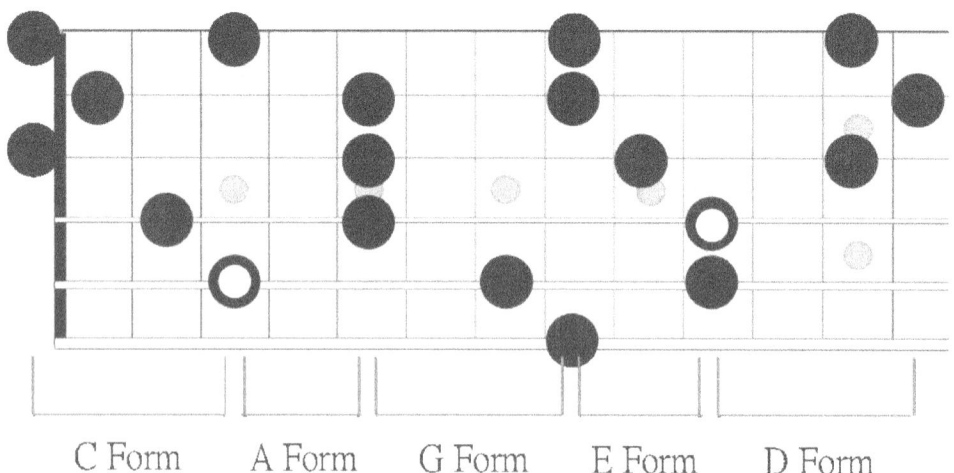

C Form　　A Form　　G Form　　E Form　　D Form

Taking these five types of string pressing method and move them horizontally to an open fret position, then you will discover there are five fingerings of chord. That is C, A, G, E and D.

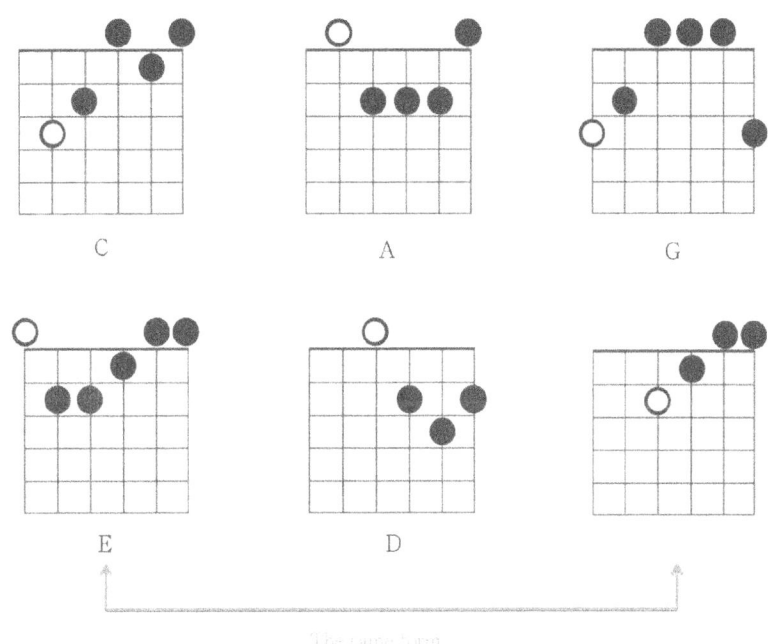

C   A   G

E   D

It is actually the identical fingering and structure.

★ If you use chord names to represent fingering, then this would often confuse people as to which chords we actually refer to. At this time, you can use numbers to represent fingerings and think, and this then would be less confusing. For instance, E fingering is used for a C chord on the 8th fret, and in other words, C chord uses fingering NO.4 on the eighth fret.

♦ Minor Third Chord

A minor third chord fingering directly uses these fingerings for variations, by changing the 3rd note of every major third chord to $^b3$.

And then to correct the fingerings which are not smooth for playing:

C Transform	A Transform	G Transform
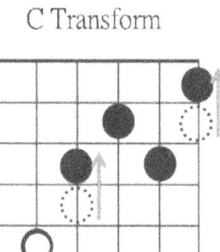	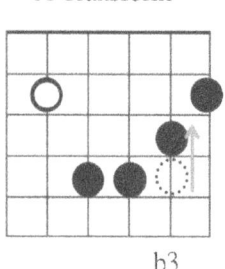	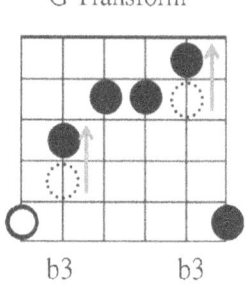
b3 b3	b3	b3 b3

E Transform	D Transform
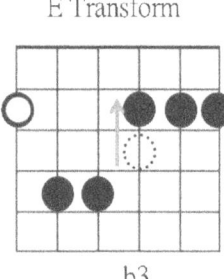	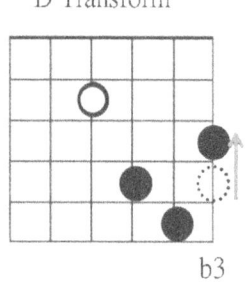
b3	b3

Correction of C fingering Change. Omit root on the 5th string.

Correction of G fingering Change. Pressing the 2nd string as the 5th note and omit the 1st string.

C Transform Fixed	G Transform Fixed
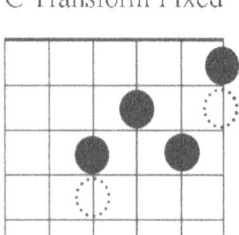	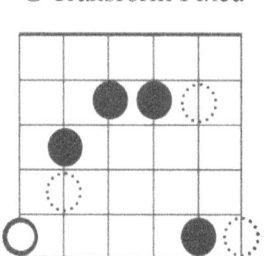

◆Ascending Chord Root and Scale Graphic

An ascending scale chord uses musical notes in a scale in an orderly basis, and is formed by piling up with an interval of a third. Root on a guitar fretboard is mostly placed on the 4th, 5th and 6th strings; thus, we only need to list out those scale positions for root.

Selections for the most often seen root position are as below:

(1) Starting from the 6th string (The graphic is in A key)

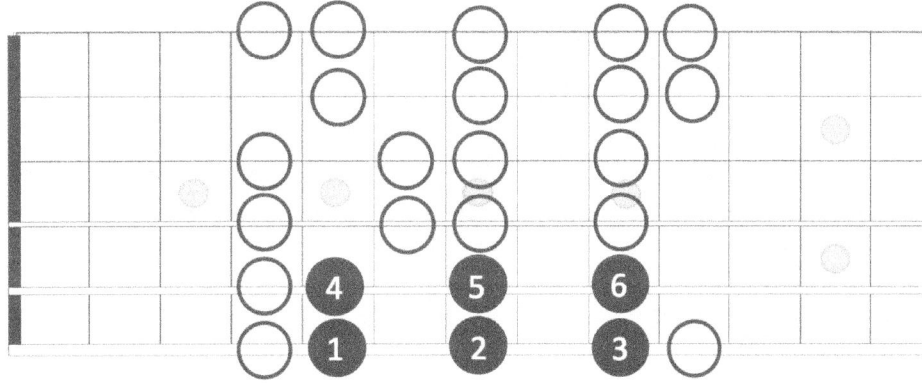

(2) Stating from the 5th string (The graphic is in D key)

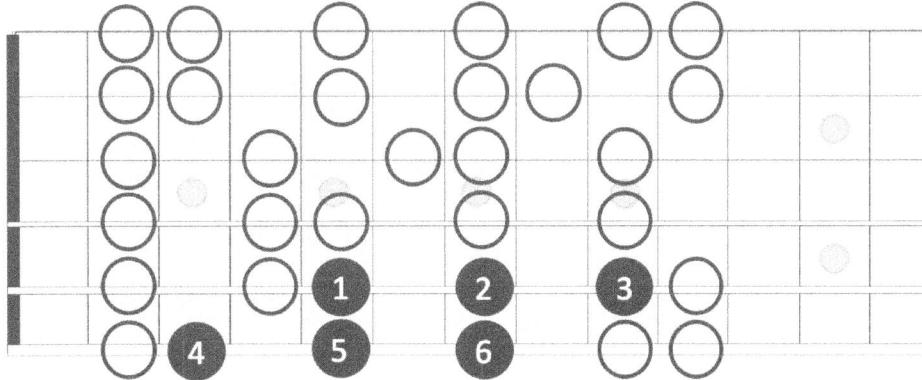

★ The selection of chord fingering often uses E and A fingerings an index finger pressing on.

Let's see the most often used playing methods mentioned above (1) and use of E and A fingerings:

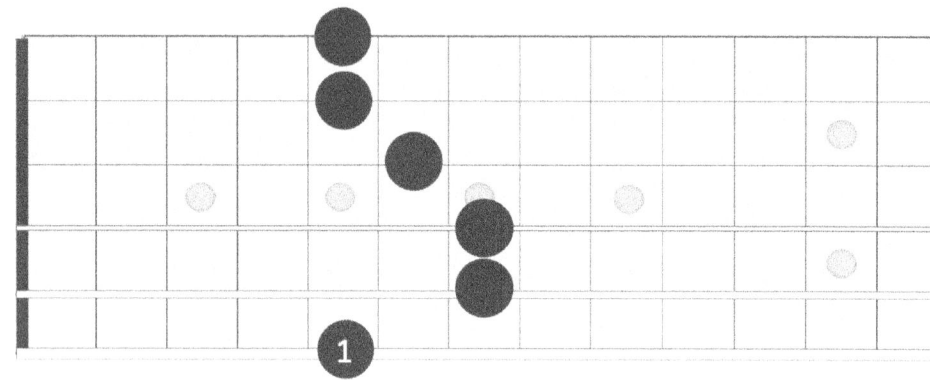

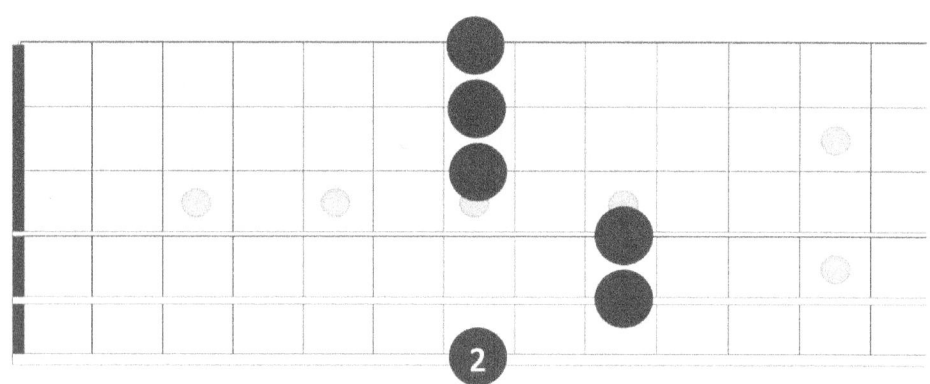

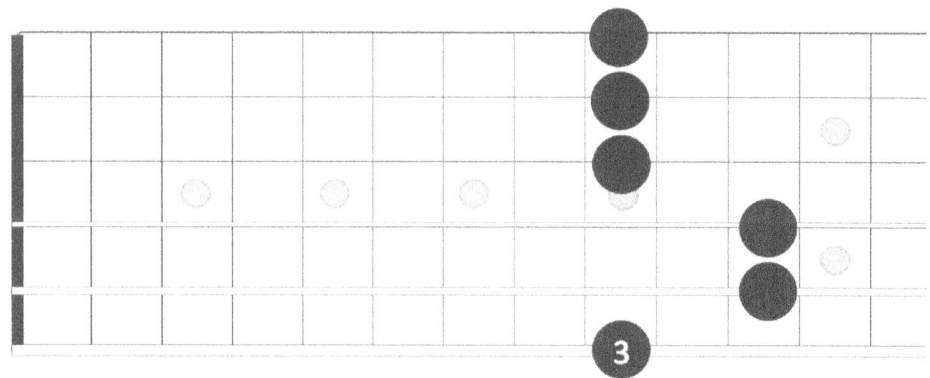

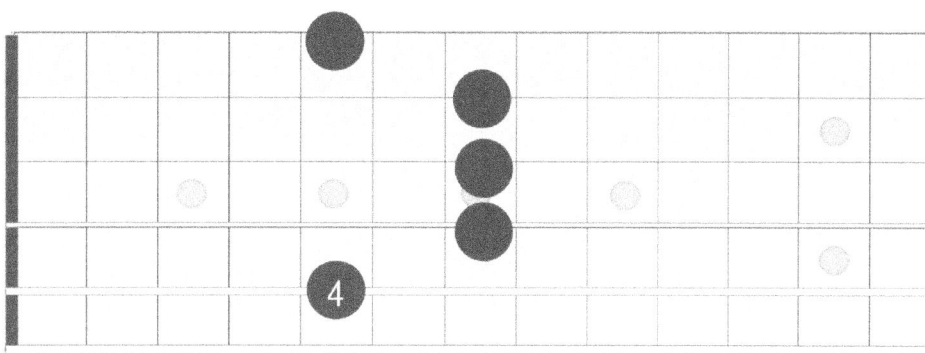

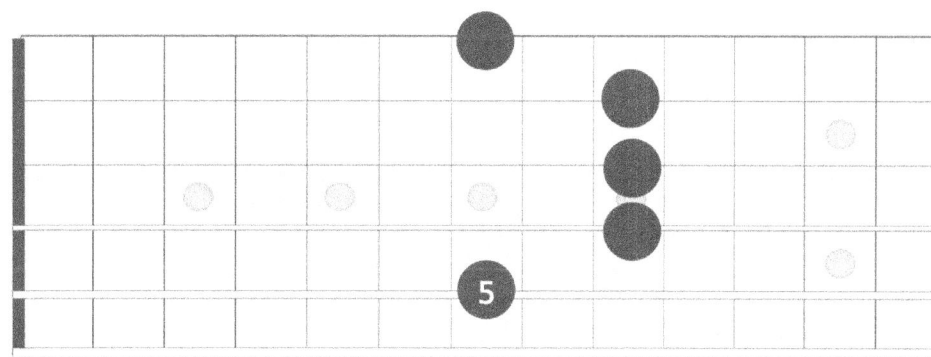

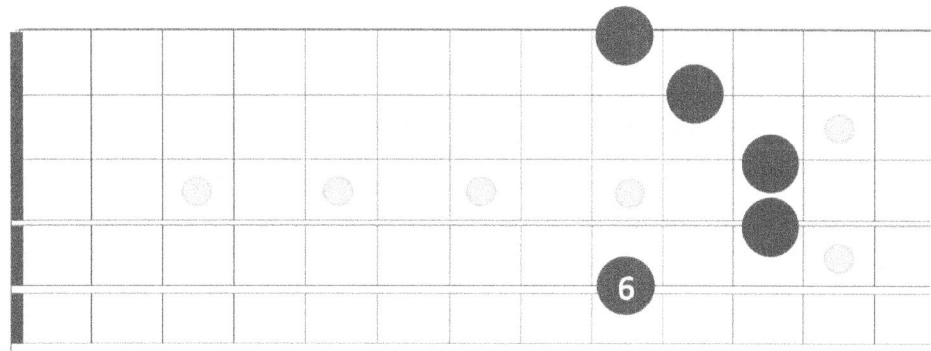

For the above playing methods, there are approximately the advantages and disadvantages below:

[Advantage] It is the easiest to press on.

[Disadvantage] It is easy for hands to be overworked, increasing chances of making mistakes, and harmony wise, it mostly belongs to a horizontal movement, and monotonous (dull).

Therefore, through understanding fingerings of the five main chords, we can think about adjusting the selection methods of chord.

[Methods of Adjustment] Taking chords locating at higher fret positions and switching to your pinky or a ring finger to press root. That is changing to a C or a G fingering.

We will individually modify chord fingerings of root 3, 5 and 6 as below:

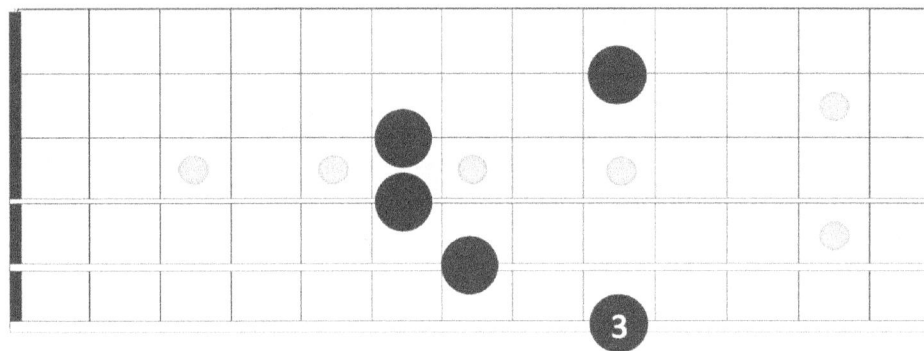

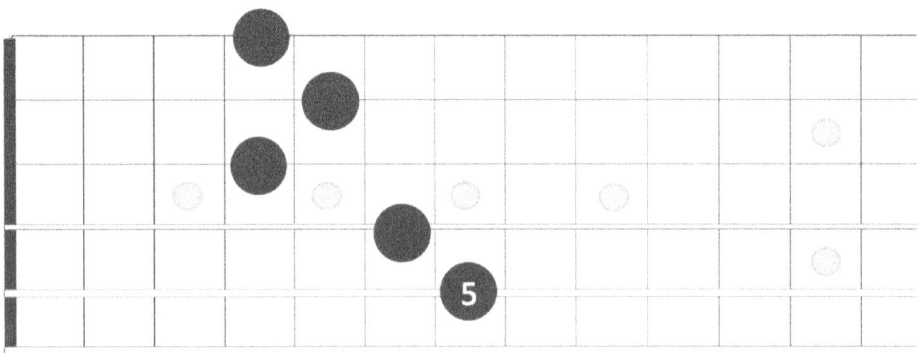

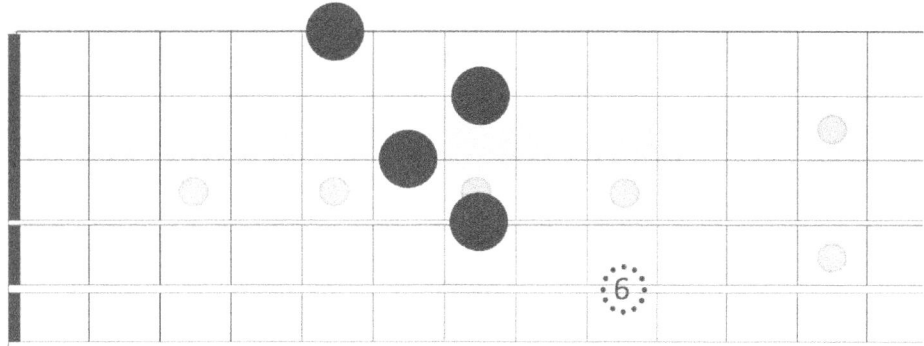

★ And certainly you may feel such chord adjustment method would still be quite difficult to play. Please allow us to provide a direction of thinking here and we can choose other types such as seventh chord, ninth chord and etc., to replace a basic triad chord. In terms of string pressing method, you would then feel much easier. And since there are many kinds of chord types, areas such as using chord types for replacement is not the focus in this handbook, therefore, it is not available here. Please rely on concepts for trials and discoveries on your own.

As for another adjustment method, in addition to changing chord fingerings, there is an addition of root position changing. If changing playing method (1) to:

[Track-30]

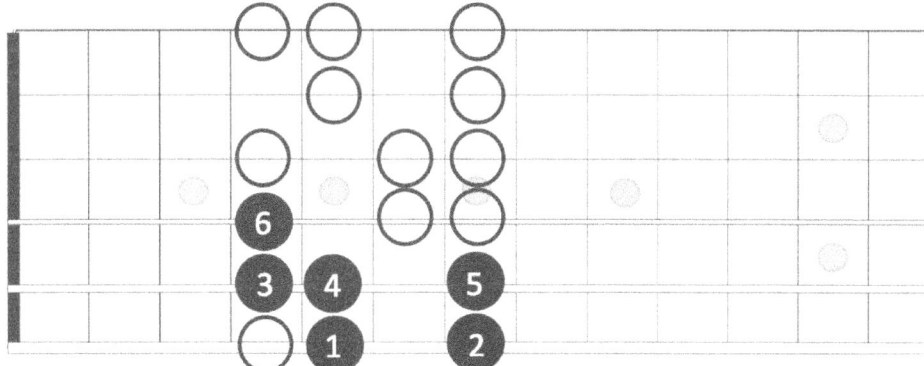

Matching with selected chords and it becomes:

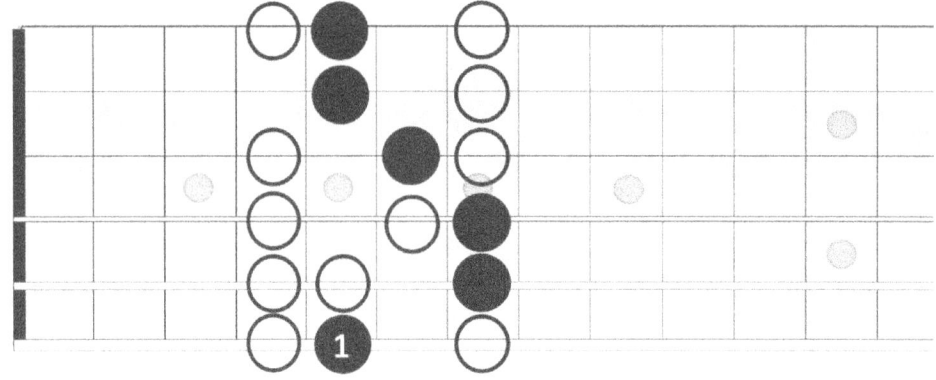

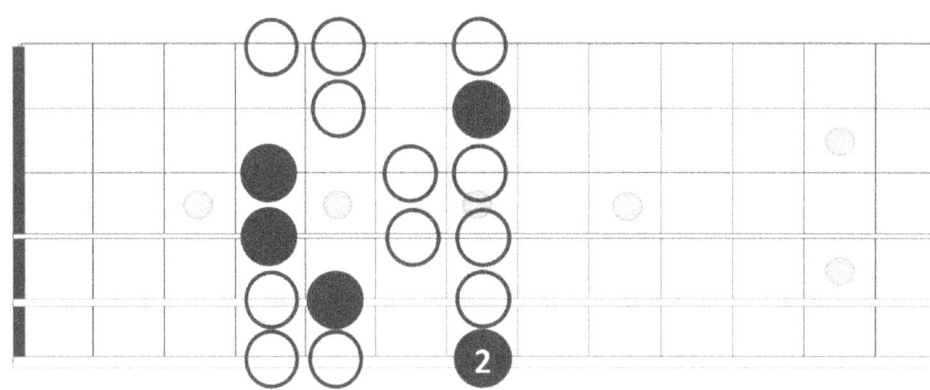

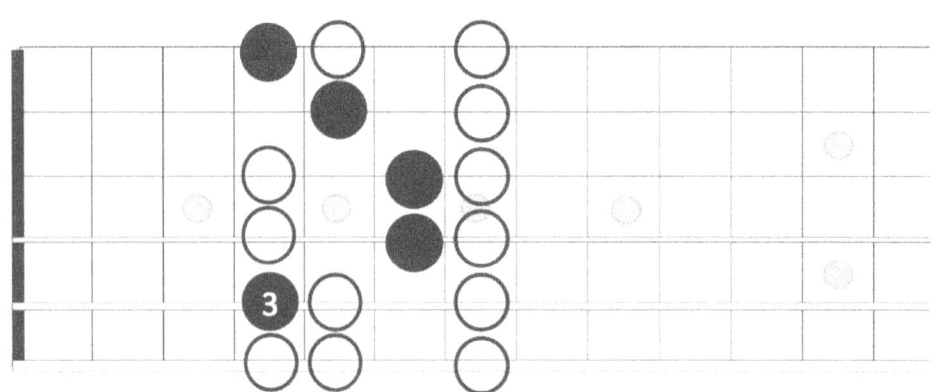

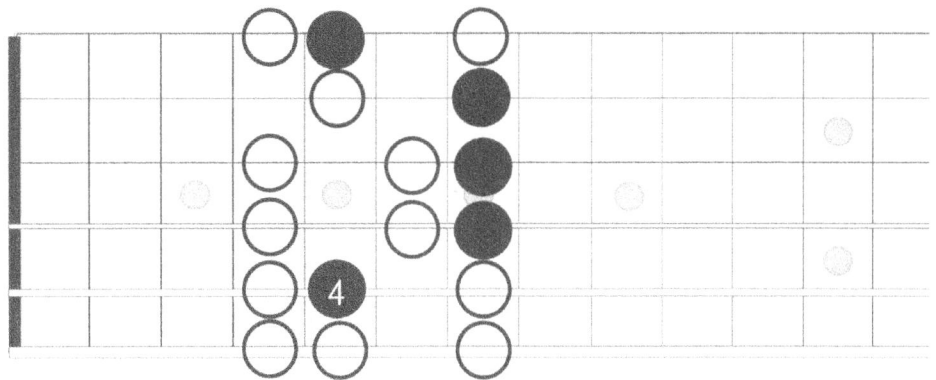

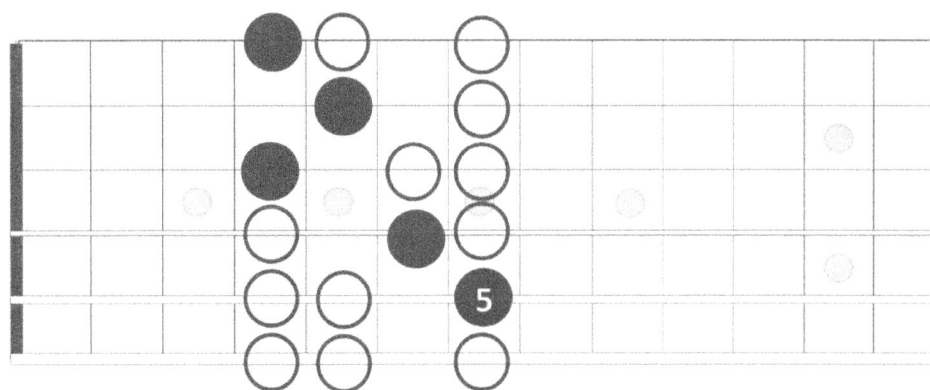

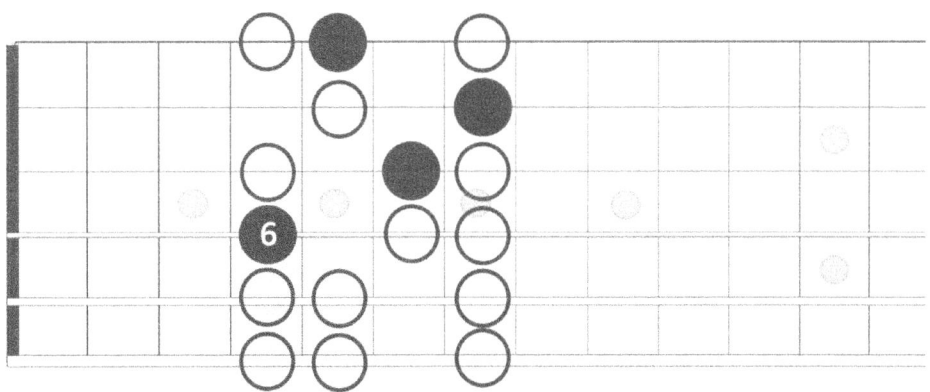

Have you discovered it now? Now a total of 6 chords are on the same pattern graphics!

This way your left hand can be more on a certain fret position, while changing chords, interval structures would have some variations. While you are playing some melodic lines, you can also play them more calmly. Certainly if you feel there are fingerings which you feel less easier to press on, you can fix them on your own!

For other arrangements of ascending scale root, you can also try choosing chord fingerings to press on!

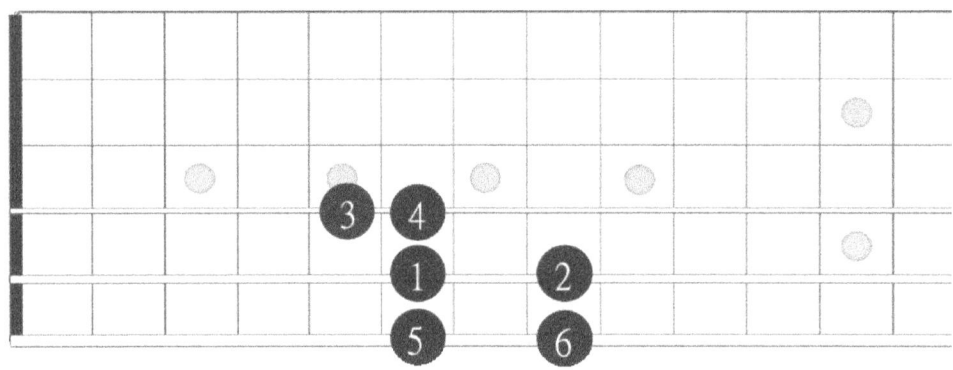

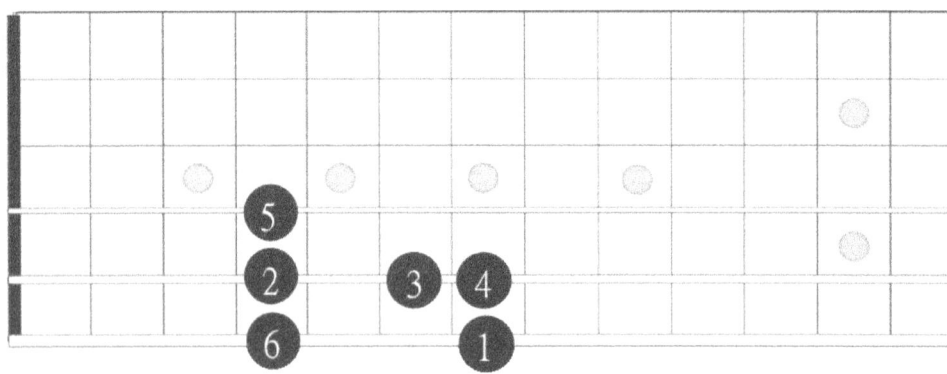

Try using this pressing method on songs which you often play.

On a guitar fretboard, due to string-pressing problems of fingers, as long as you can remember the 3rd note at the lowest position to be the first inversion, and it's often represented by a slash chord. For instance C/E chord; when the 5th note is at the lowest note, then it is a second inversion. And for instance, C/G chord and so on.

In the following section, we have individually listed out the fingerings of the 1st and the 2nd inversions of a major third and a minor third. 1 represents root, 3 represents the 3rd note in a major third, ^{b}3 represents the 3rd note in minor chord and 5 represents the 5th note. The numbers in the graphic below represent a left hand finger symbols.

♦Major Third Chord

* The Lowest Note is on the 6 String

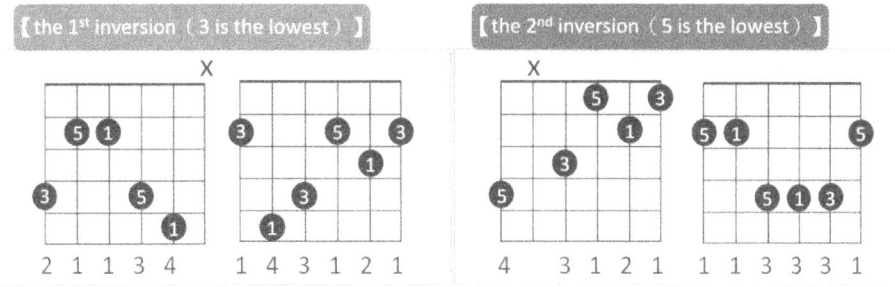

* The Lowest Note is on the 5th String

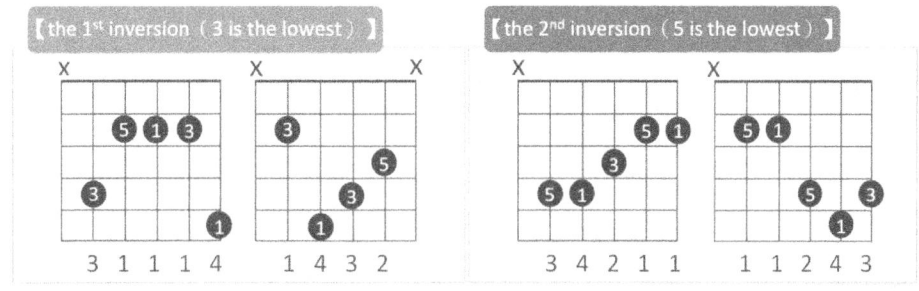

THE APPLICATIONS : Final, Enhances Practices Everywhere

* The Lowest Note is on the 4th String

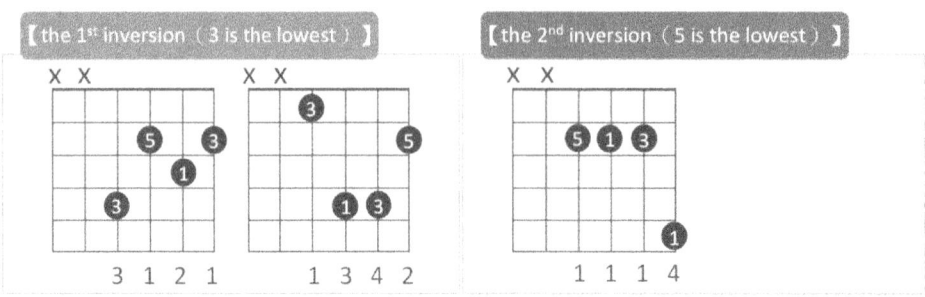

♦ Minor Third Chord

* The Lowest Note is on the 6th String

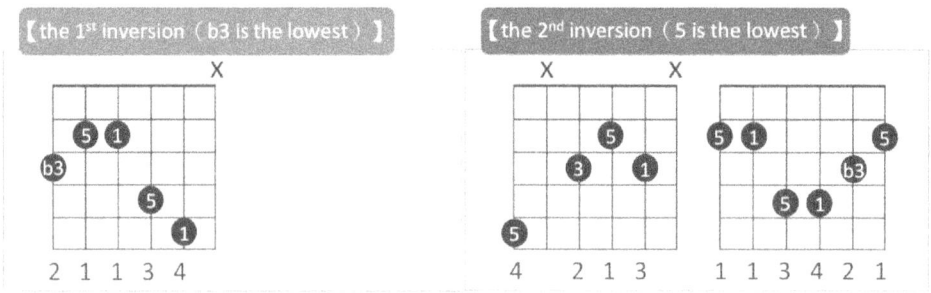

* The Lowest Note is on the 5th String

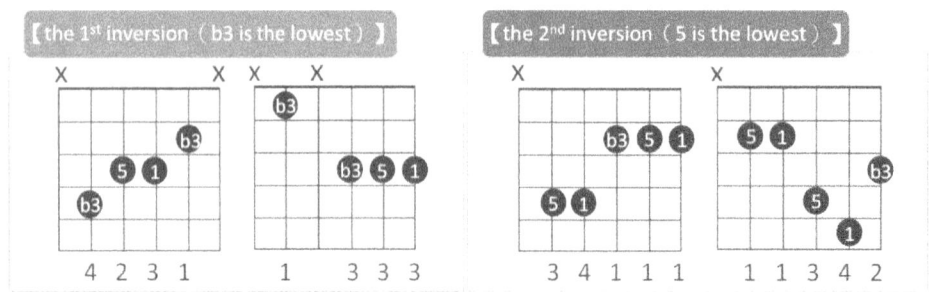

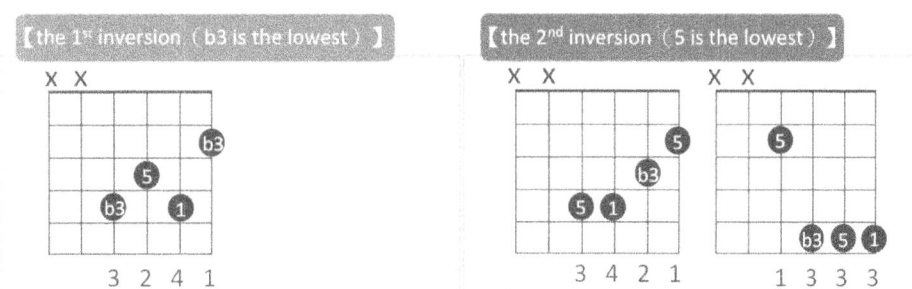

The above is a triad inversion fingering and as there are only 3 comprising notes for a triad, therefore, only two inversions are available. If it's a seventh chord (such as seventh chord, its composition would be 1 3 5 ^{b}7), then it has an additional ^{b}7 note at the lowest note of the 3rd inversion. For related chord fingerings, after you are familiar with the basic fingerings, you can self-calculate the original seventh chord as well as its inversion chords. Or you can look for available chord books for references.

1. In chord progressions, first let's analyzes the comprising note in the previous or a later chords (for instance C chord: C E G, Am chord: ACE).

2. Placing the same notes in comprising notes as the lowest notes to proceed playing (for example: when a C chord connects to an Am chord, Am uses C as the lowest note, and that is the first inversion of Am to play). If there is no identical notes, then you would find a comprising note and place it as the lowest note which is nearest to current bass note (such as G chord GBD as well as B note being placed as the lowest note and connects back to a C chord), such as the examples below:

[Track-31]

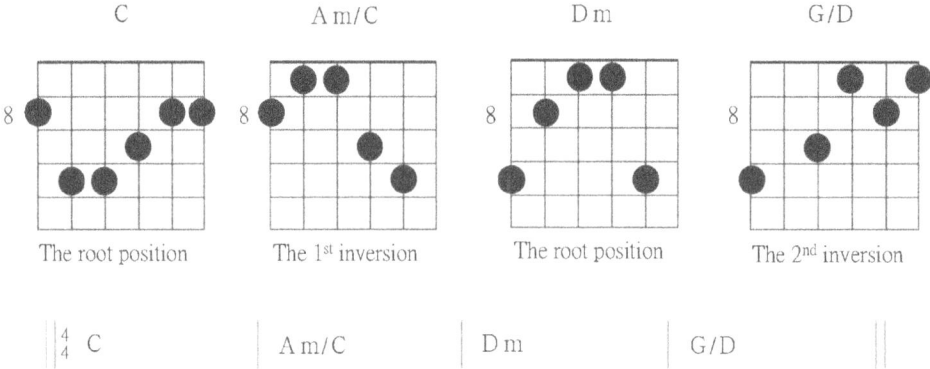

C	Am/C	Dm	G/D
The root position	The 1st inversion	The root position	The 2nd inversion

$\frac{4}{4}$ C   Am/C   Dm   G/D

This way, have you discovered that the performance fret positions have become more stable after using inversion chords? For more uses and methods of inversion chords, you can refer to my other publication work "*Your Training Notebook On Pop Music Special Chord Progressions*".

When we can use the original + inversion chords to allow our hands to be fixed on a certain fret position for playing, it then becomes convenient for us to add some fill-ins in the performance.

◆1. First find a building block graphic which belongs to chords on fret positions

In ordering to combine with a scale building block graphic, comprising musical notes of a chord will need to adopt scale numbered musical notations to express so it can be clearer.

Ascending Scale Chord Series	Comprising Notes (Numbered Musical Notation)
I	1、3、5
II	2、4、6
III	3、5、7
IV	4、6、1
V	5、7、2
VI	6、1、3
VII	7、2、4

In an ascending chord, the I, IV and V series are major 3rd chords, and that is the comprising format is the same. Therefore, you can use the same major 3rd chord fingering; and II, III, VI series is a minor 3rd chord, and that means you can use the same minor third chord fingering. Thus, for the 5 types of basic major third chord fingering which we have listed out previously, in a scale of a certain key, they can be I series chord for use and they can also be IV or V series chord for use.

* <u>Major Third Chord</u>

Taking C fingering as one example, when you use this fingering to play I, IV and V chords in C key, their individual positions in a scale pattern are:

★ Numbers in the graphics below are scale numbers of numbered musical notations, not the numbers in chord comprising note format.

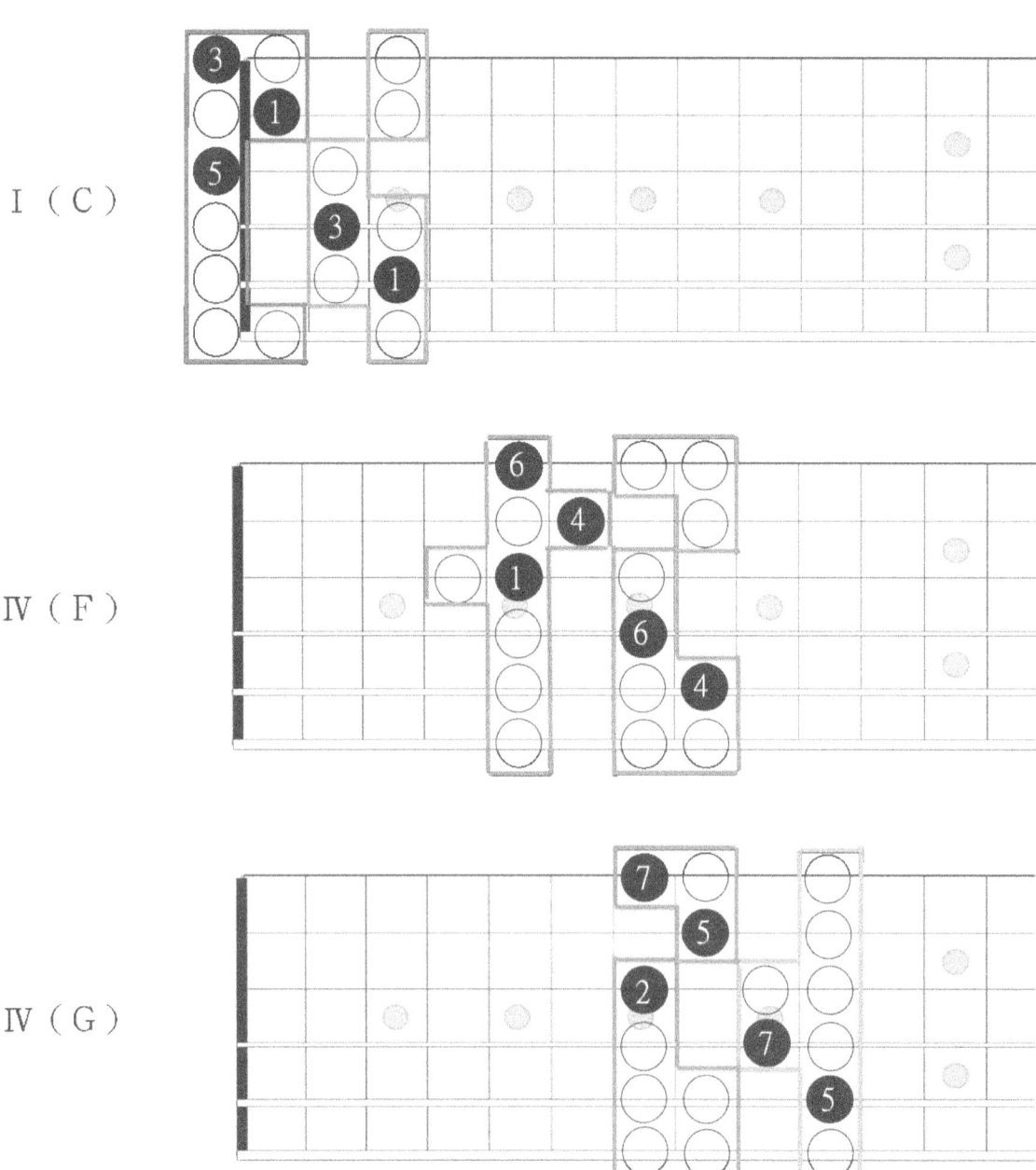

I（C）

IV（F）

IV（G）

Do you see that? Although the chord fingering looks identical, it is actually a different chord and the individual building blocks, which they belong to, are different. At this time, you need to memorize, to be more familiar with scale building block positions which each chord series belongs to via practices.

There are 5 types of basic chord fingering for one chord, in order to understand I, IV, and V series chords to a relative position of a scale pattern graphic, there are 15 graphics for you to comprehend slowly! This sounds quite intimidating, but it's actually not that bad as it's just placing the fingering in different scale building block graphics. If you don't have a guitar in hand, then you can try drawing it on a piece of paper. When you have a guitar, then you can look at the graphics and play along, and you will be more familiar slowly. In addition to allowing your fingers to be more familiar with fingerings, it is more important to remember comprising notes of chords as well as positions of other musical notes. When you know what notes to play upon performing time, you will be less likely to make mistakes upon improvisations, and this would sound more beautiful!

* Minor Third Chord

Taking the 4th fingering as an example, when you use this fingering to play II, III, and VI chords in C key, their individual positions in a scale are:

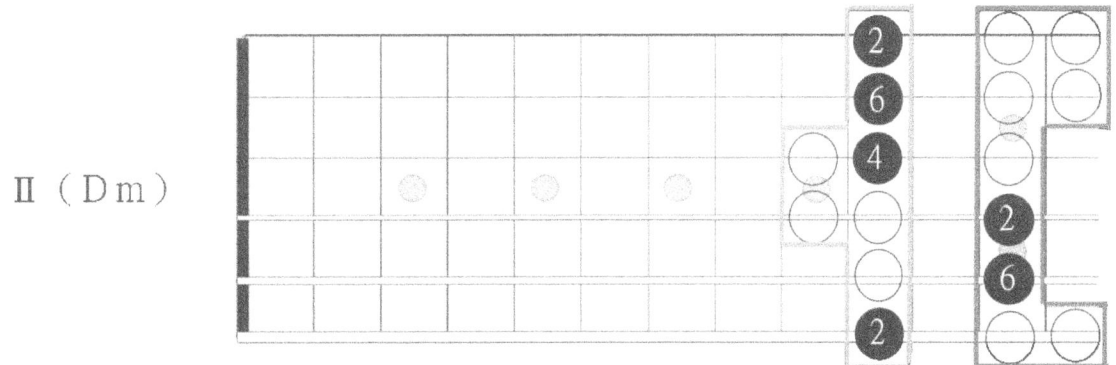

II (Dm)

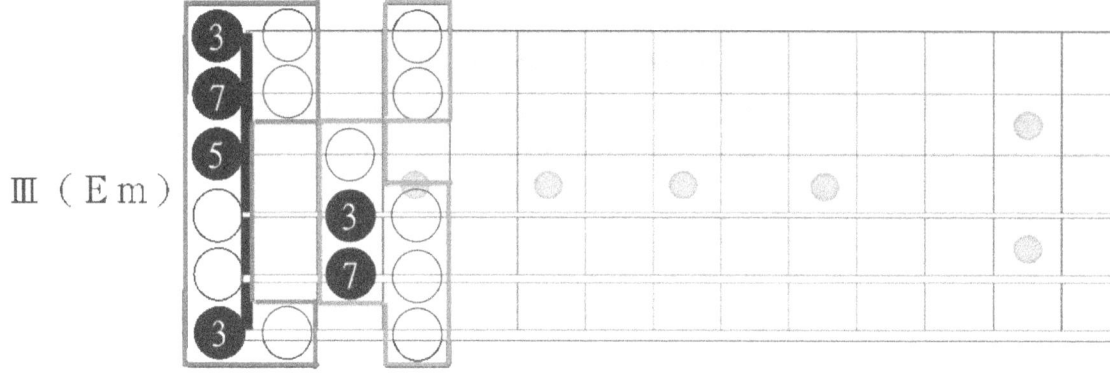

III（Em）

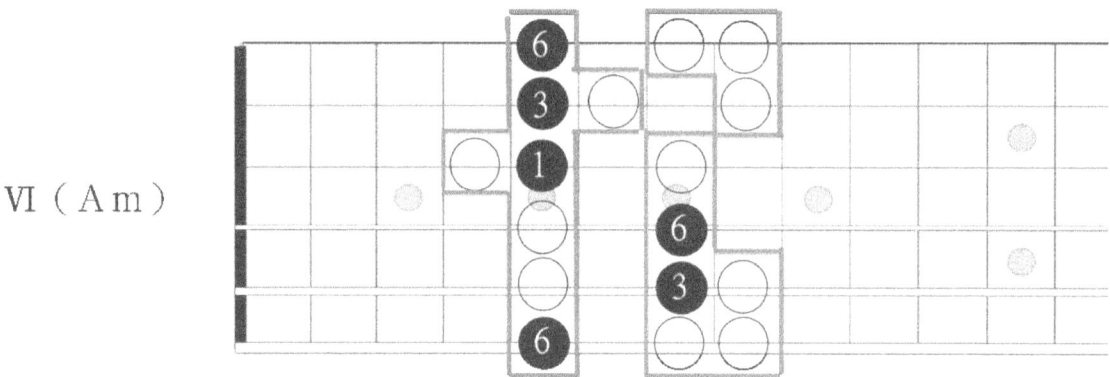

VI（Am）

Similarly, one minor third has basic 5 fingerings which allows II, III and VI series to be used individually. Therefore, you will also need to be familiar with their positions on scale pattern graphics individually!

* And remember there are inversion chord sections which you should practice!

To be familiar with scale graphics, to practice directly is also the fastest method, but please remember you should think about it in your head upon practice.

◆2. Add fill-ins

Upon pressing on chords, you need to know what position in a scale you are currently at so you can proceed to performance immediately without thinking about where the notes you would like to play when entering single note melodies. On the contrary, it is the same. Let's see an example on a chord plus fill-ins:

<1> (A Key)

[Track-32]

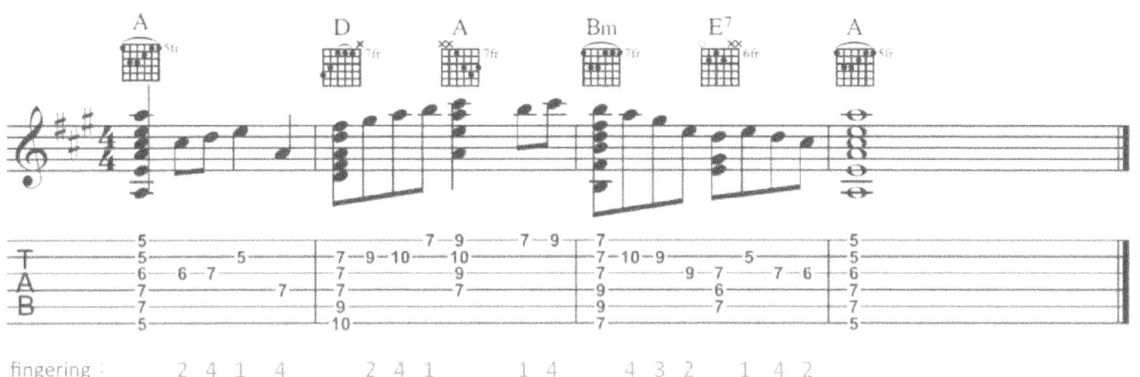

Possibly people may ask, why do we choose this fingering for D in the 2nd measure?

Here's a simple answer: "it's easy to play."

If we just look at the pressing methods of chord, you may probably feel that it's not easy to play at all; however, if you consider notes in those melodies in the back, and the following A chord as well as its matching pressing method to the highest note. You would still need to use this chord fingering which gives more fluency in melodic connections.

Certainly, we can use the fingering below to press D chord, which is quite easy to press on. However, by doing so, D chord part only has 3 comprising notes remained, and after deducting melodic notes, there's only root and its octave left. Aurally, it sounds duller.

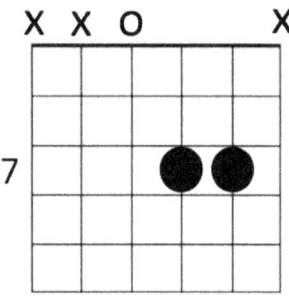

<2> (D key)

[Track-33]

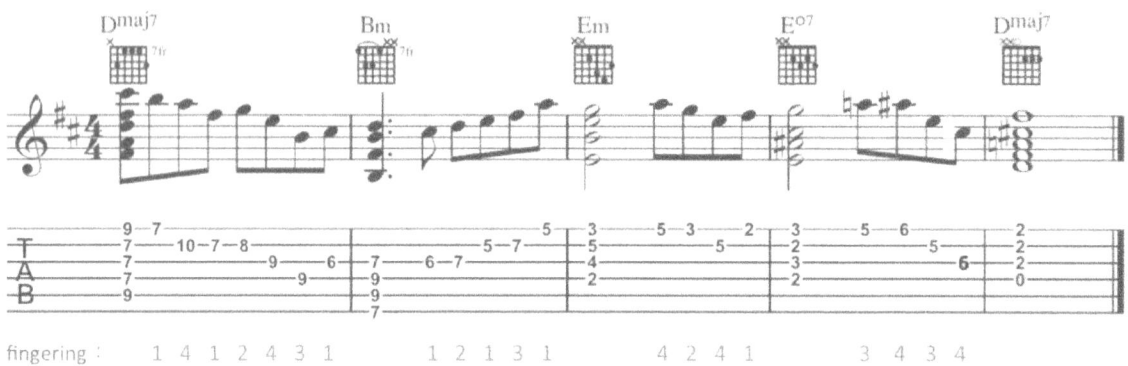

<3> (A key)

This example of practice is a small musical performance work, using the techniques of the above chords plus scale melody, and what is different from the previous examples is that an inversion chord is used this time, and this allows the bass to have a little melodic lines itself. This is a technique used by guitar performance which is similar to Chord Melody in Jazz guitar, please try to experience more of this.

[Track-34]

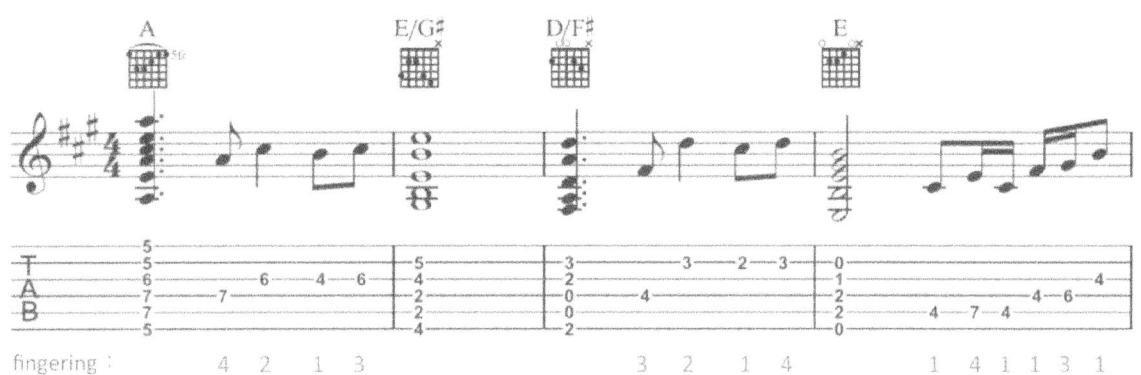

fingering :

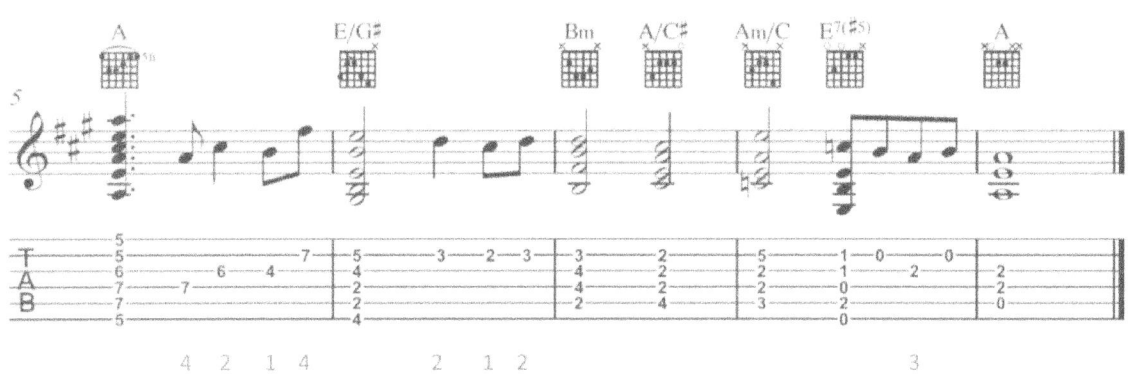

Chapter TEN

Arpeggios which Add Melodic Tastes

A chord arpeggio actually is to use chord comprising notes and play them directly, and this is slightly different from fingerpicking performance broken chords. Broken chord is mainly for accompanying use and melodic quality is quite weak. Arpeggios however, are also being placed in between melodic lines, adding colors to chords which they belong to.

In addition to increasing performance techniques (for instance, strumming and tapping), arpeggios are also very suitable for being used as a tool to be familiar with a fretboard. Here we use a basic triad arpeggio to start an explanation.

When practicing arpeggios, similarly, you can also use 5 types of basic chord in the previous chapter as a basis, and plus the comprising notes which you haven't pressed on, then they become complete arpeggios.

♦ Major Third Chord Arpeggios

C Fingering : (1, 3 and 5 refer to the format of root, 3rd and 5th notes of chord comprising notes.)

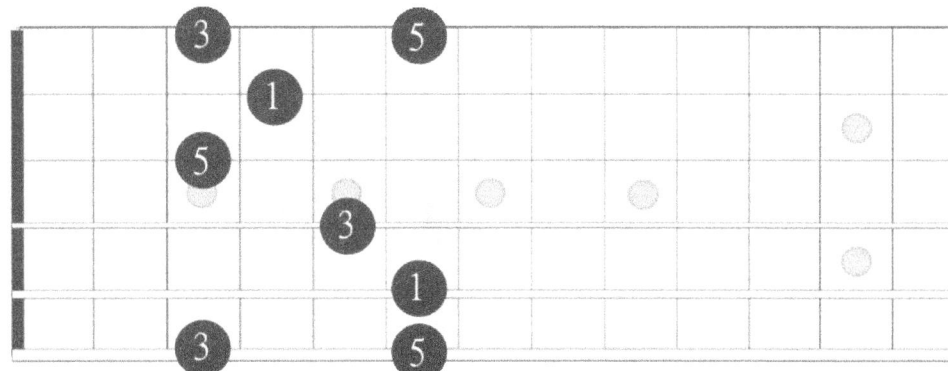

THE APPLICATIONS : Final, Enhances Practices Everywhere

<1>

fingering : 4 3 1 3 4 3 1 2   1 4 1 2 1 2 1 3   1 3 4 3 4 3 1 3   4

<2>

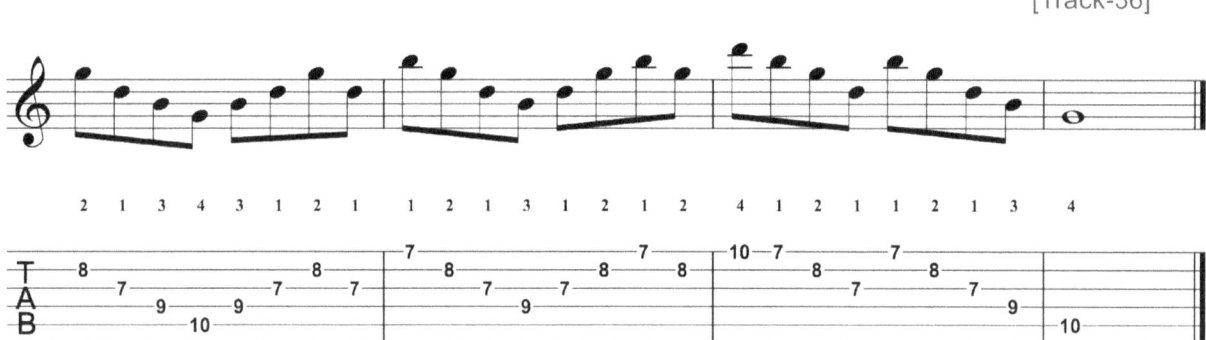

A Fingering :

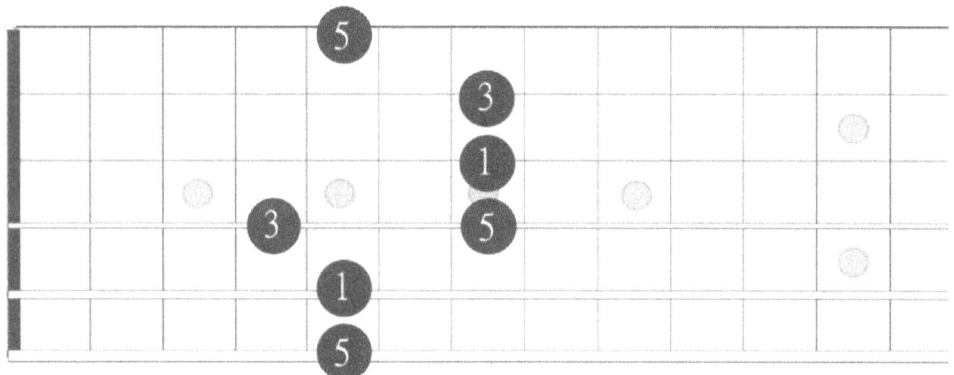

<1>

[Track-37]

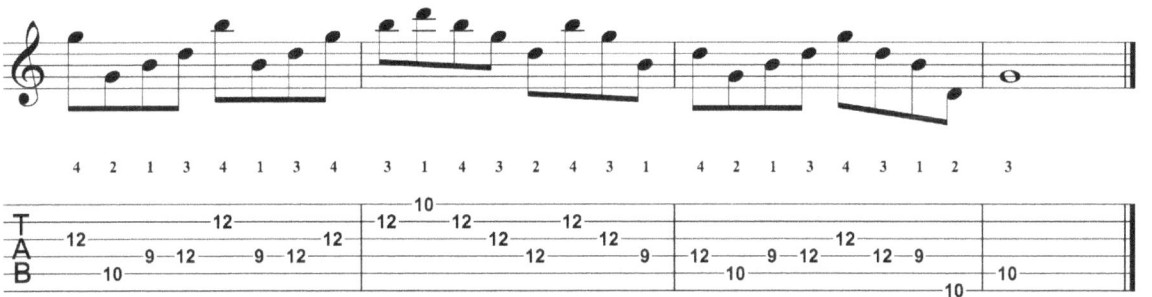

fingering : 2 1 4 3 4 1 4 3   2 4 3 2 1 4 3 1   2 1 2 1 3 4 3 1   2

<2>

[Track-38]

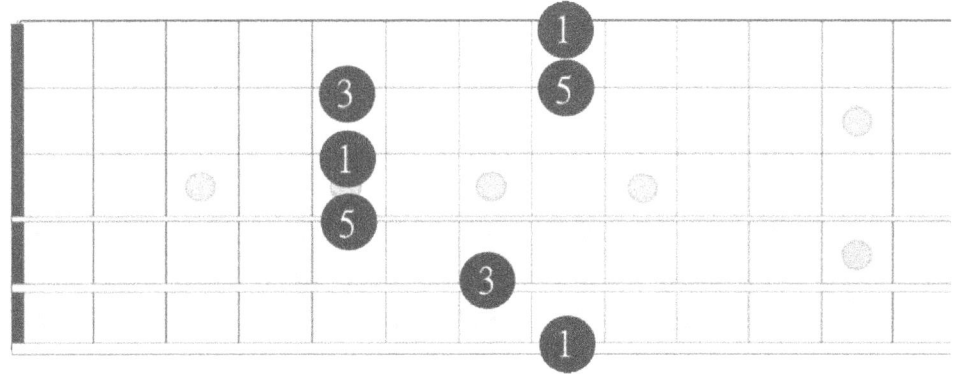

G Fingering :

 is above, fingerboard diagram below.

THE APPLICATIONS : Final, Enhances Practices Everywhere

<1>

[Track-39]

fingering : 4 3 1 1 1 4 4 4   1 1 1 3 1 1 3 1   4 1 1 1 1 1 1 3   4

<2>

[Track-40]

4 1 1 4 1 1 1 1   1 3 1 1 4 1 1 1   3 4 3 1 1 1 4 1   4

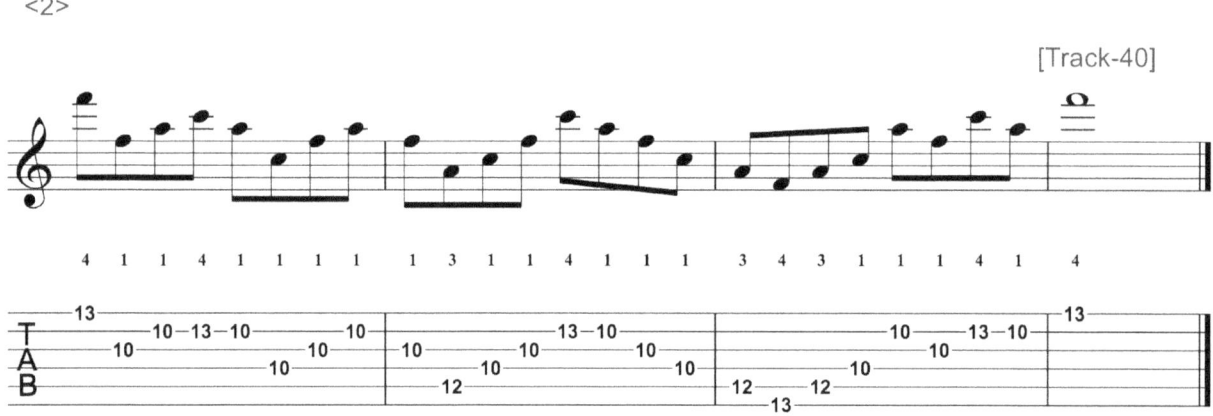

E Fingering :

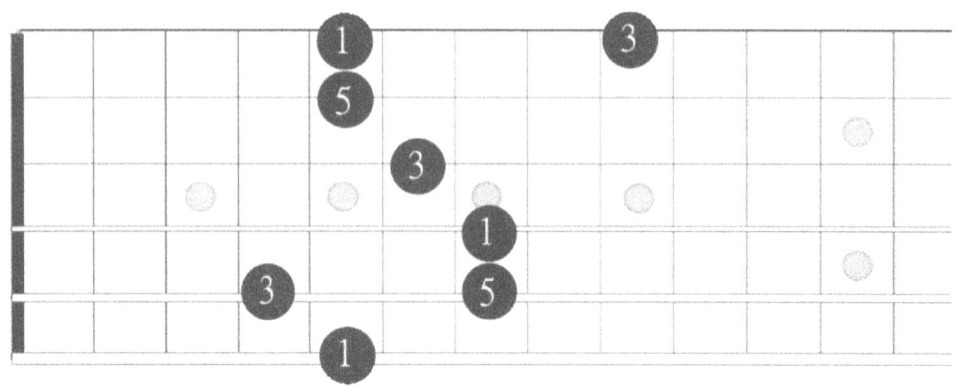

<1>

[Track-41]

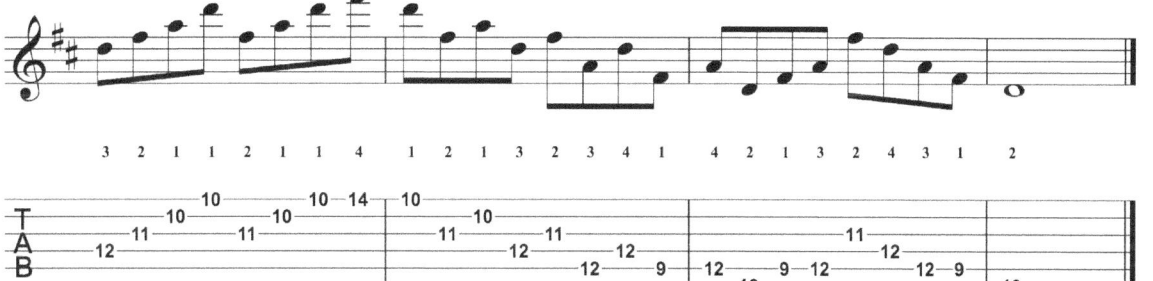

fingering :   2 1 3 4 2 1 1 4   1 1 2 4 3 1 3 4   2 4 3 2 4 3 1 4   2

<2>

[Track-42]

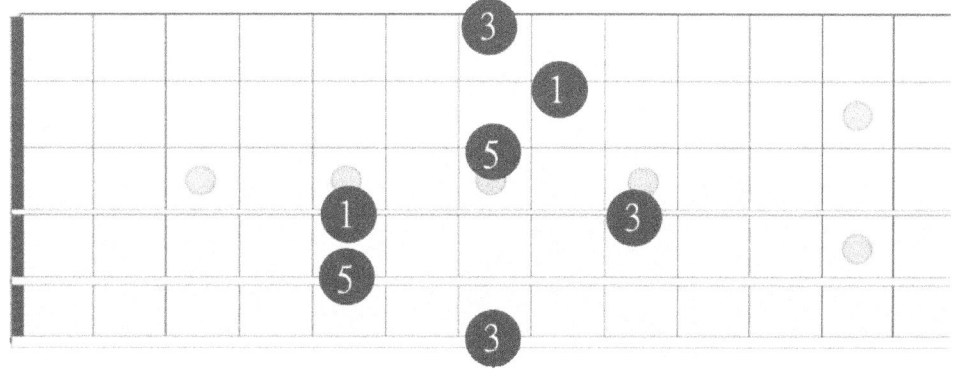

3 2 1 1 2 1 1 4   1 2 1 3 2 3 4 1   4 2 1 3 2 4 3 1   2

D Fingering :

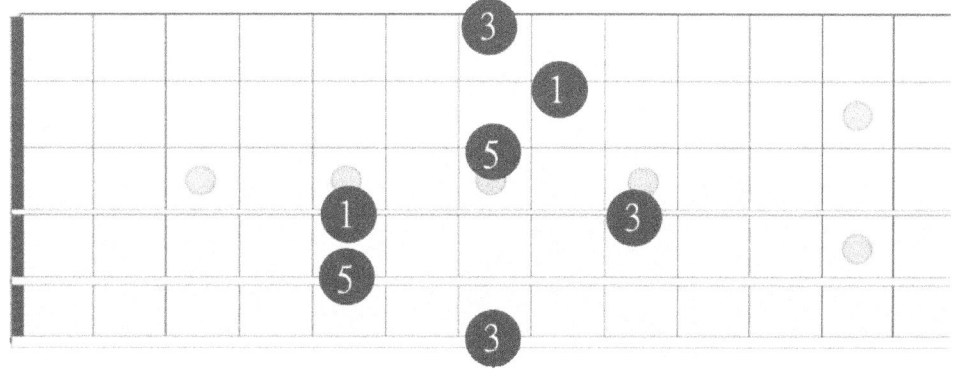

<1>

[Track-43]

fingering : 1 1 3 1 1 4 1 1   1 4 2 3 2   3 2 4   3 2 4 1 2 4 1 1   1

<2>

[Track-44]

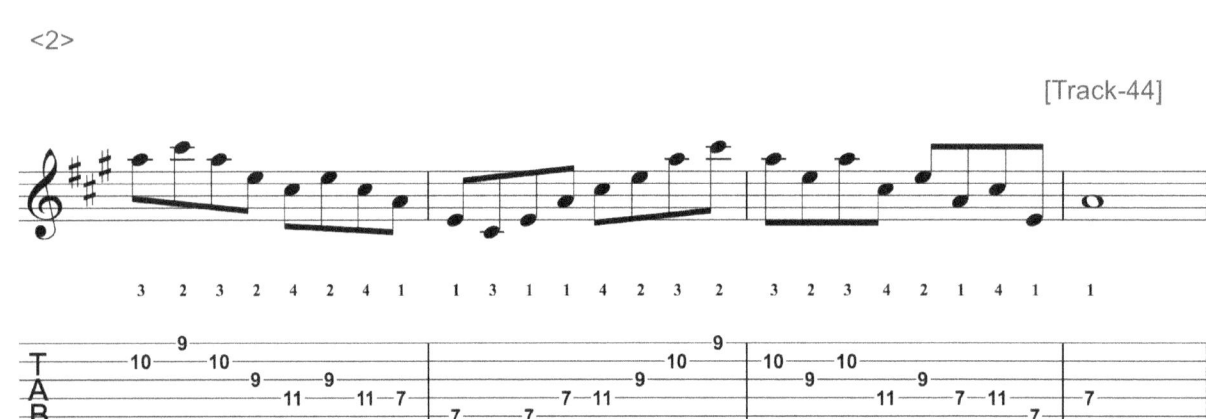

<u>C Fingering Change</u>: (1, [b]3 and 5 refer to the format of root, 3rd and 5th notes of chord comprising note.)

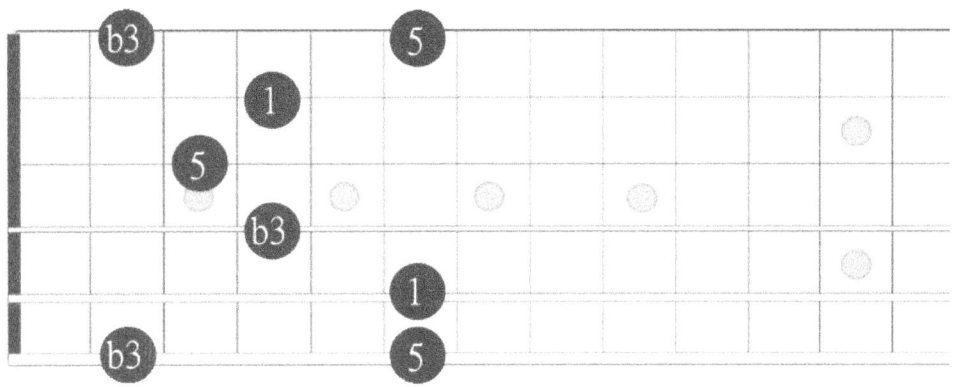

<1>

[Track-45]

fingering :   4   3   1   3   4   2   1   2   1   4   1   2   1   2   1   2   4   3   4   2   1   2   4   3   4

<2>

[Track-46]

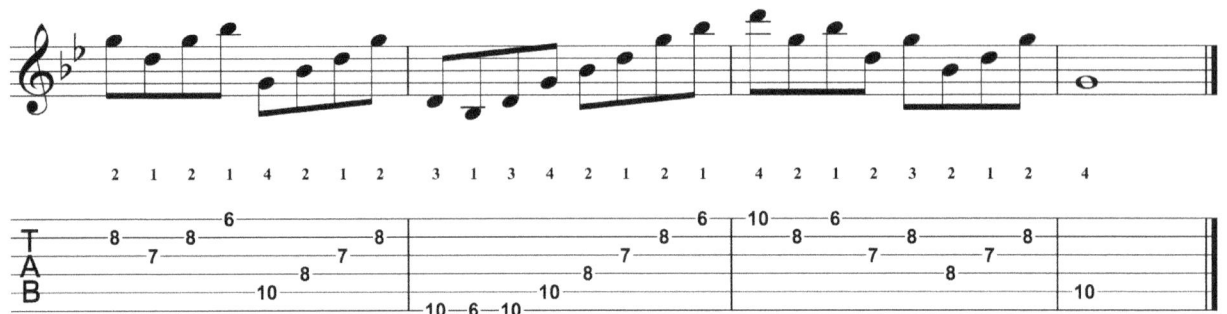

A Fingering Change:

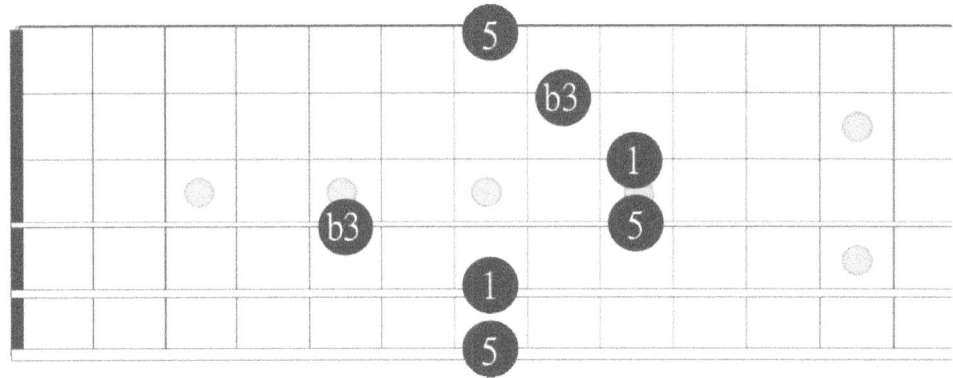

<1>

[Track-47]

fingering : 2 1 4 3 2 1 2 4   3 2 4 3 1 4 3 1   2 1 2 1 4 1 2 1   2

<2> (We can change the ^b3 on 4th string to the ^b3 on 5th string for easier playing.)

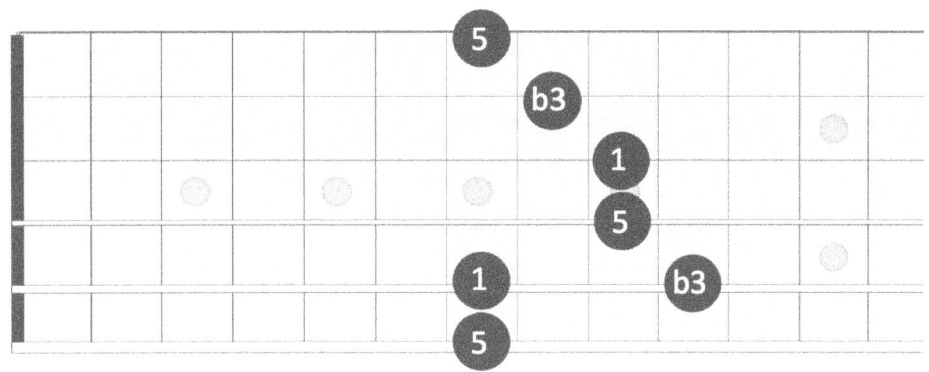

[Track-48]

1 3 4 1 1 4 3 3   4 1 4 3 3 3 2 3   2 1 3 2 3 2 4 2   1

G Fingering Change:

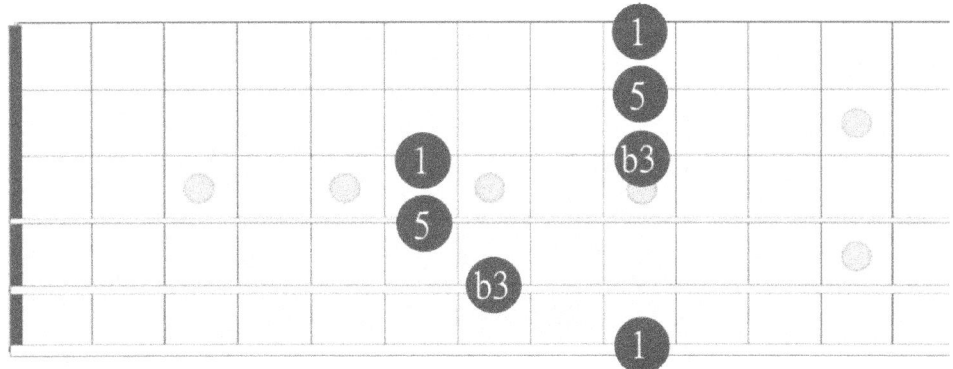

<1>

[Track-49]

fingering :   4 2 1 1 4 1 1 3   4 4 4 3 1 4 3 1   1 2 1 1 4 1 1 2   4

<2>

[Track-50]

4 1 2 1 1 4 1 4   3 4 4 3 1 4 3 1   1 2 4 2 1 1 4 3   1

E Fingering Change:

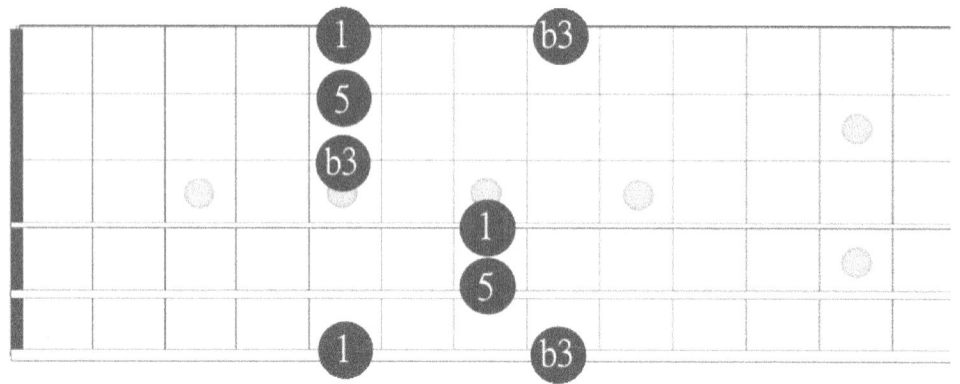

<1>

fingering : 1 4 3 3 1 1 1 4   1 1 1 3 1 1 1 3   2 3 1 1 1 3 3 4   1

<2>

3 1 1 1 4 1 1 1   1 1 3 1 1 3 2 1   3 2 3 1 1 1 3 4   1

<u>D Fingering Change</u>:

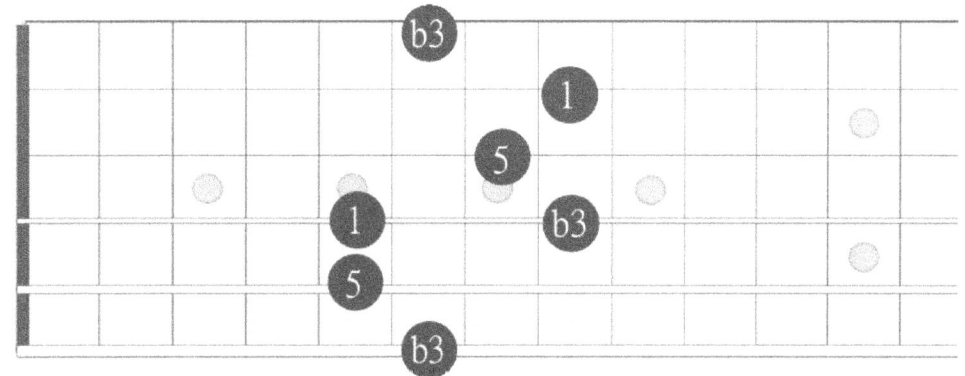

THE APPLICATIONS : Final, Enhances Practices Everywhere

<1>

[Track-53]

fingering : 1 1 2 1 1 1 1 4   3 4 2 4 3 4 3 4   1 1 2 1 1 1 4 3 4   1

<2>

[Track-54]

1 4 3 4 1 3 4 1   1 2 1 1 4 1 4 3   4 2 3 4 3 4 2 3   1

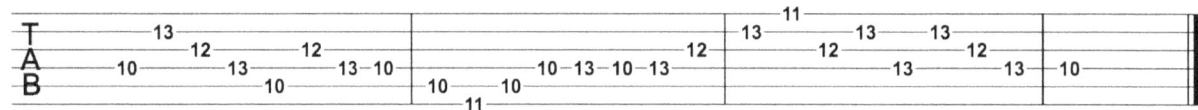

It is like the chord section in the previous chapter, one chord arpeggio has 5 types of basic fingering. In order to understand the relative positions to scale graphics of I, IV, V series arpeggios, there are 15 graphics which you need to be slowly familiar with, and similarly, there are 15 graphics for II, III, and VI series.

And about arpeggio practices, you can also use practices to connect each scale building block graphic.

1. Major Third Chord Arpeggio Connections (when I series chord arpeggio is used as an example)

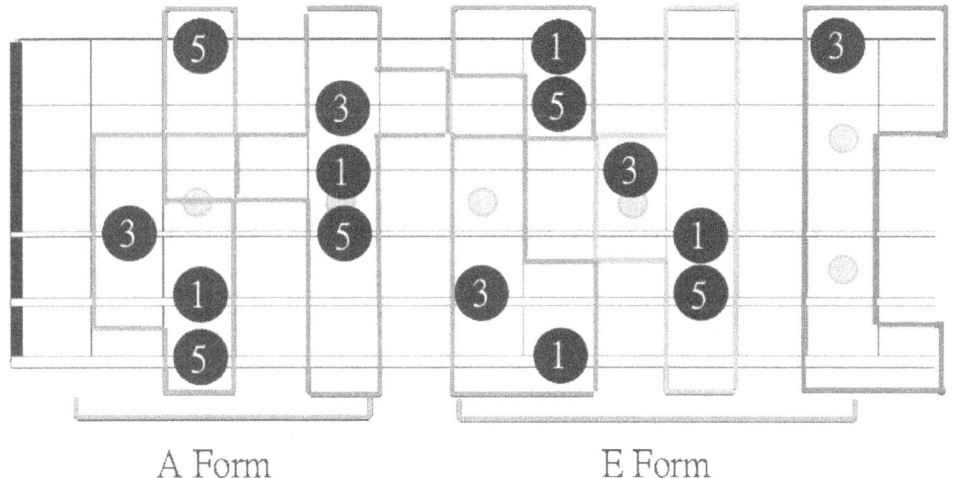

A Form   E Form

<a>

[Track-55]

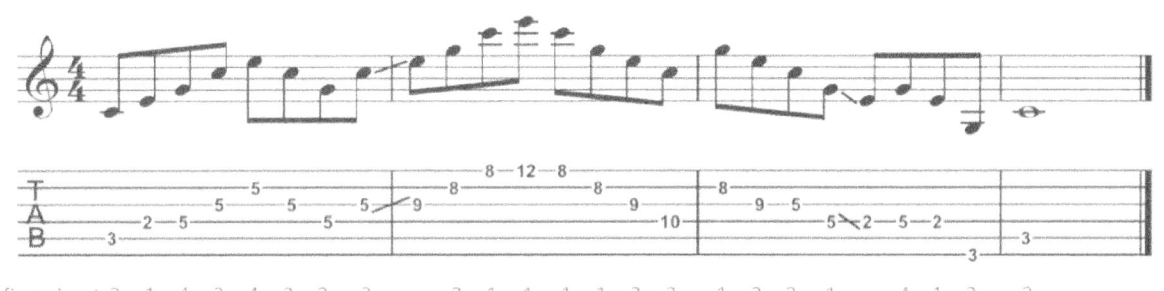

fingering : 2 1 4 3 4 3 2 3   2 1 4 1 1 2 3 1 2 2 1   4 1 2 3

<b>

[Track-56]

fingering : 1 4 1 1 2 1 1 2   3 1 2   3 2 1 3   2 1   4 3 4 3 1 2

2. Minor chord arpeggio connections (When VI series chord arpeggio is used as an example)

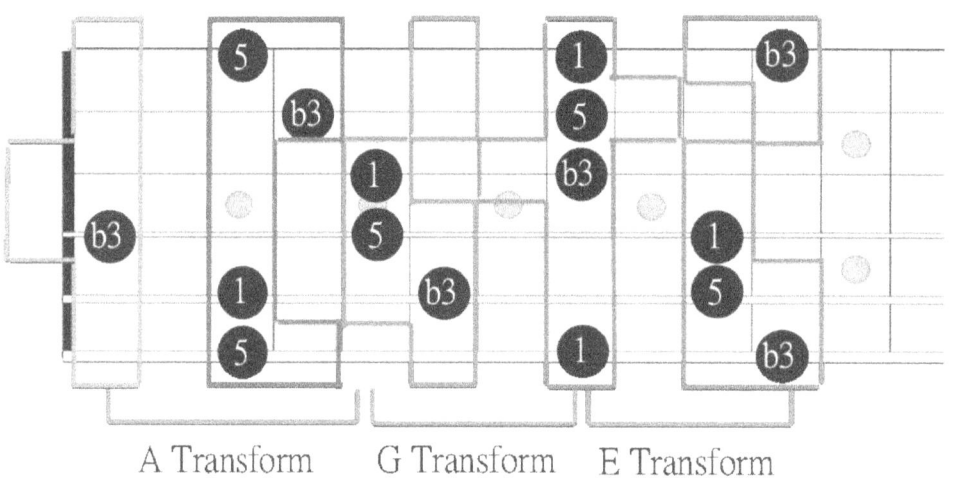

A Transform   G Transform   E Transform

<a>

[Track-57]

fingering : 1 3 2 3   2 3 1   4 1 2   1 1 4 1   4 1 1 2   1 3 1 1

<b>

fingering : 1 2 3 2 3 1 3 2   4 1 1 1 4 3 2   1 1 4 1 1 1 3 2   3 1 2 3 1

3. Use arpeggio chord progression to perform at a certain fret position, like the examples below.

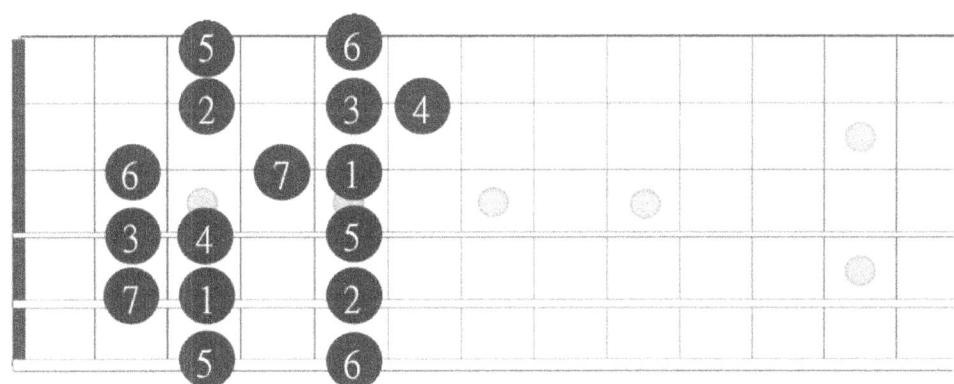

<a>

fingering : 2 1 2 1 3 4 3 1   4 1 4 3 2 1 2 1   4 3 2 1 3 4 3 1   2

THE APPLICATIONS : Final, Enhances Practices Everywhere

<b>

[Track-60]

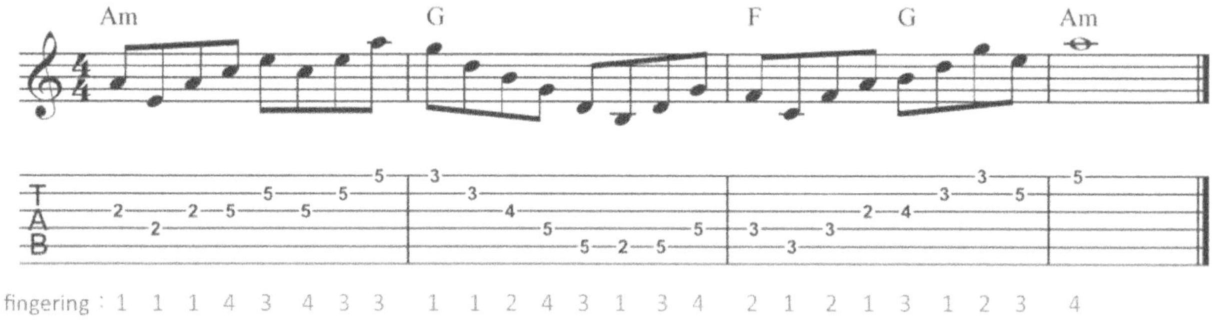

4. Use arpeggios to connect melodic lines of high and low fret positions.

<a>

[Track-61]

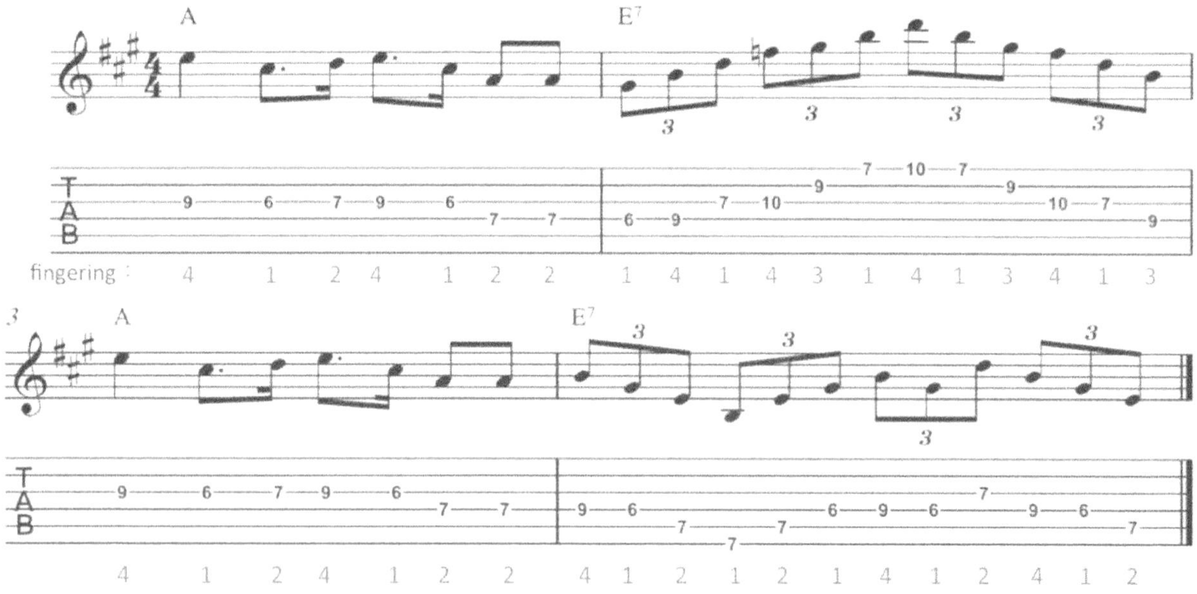

<b>

[Track-62]

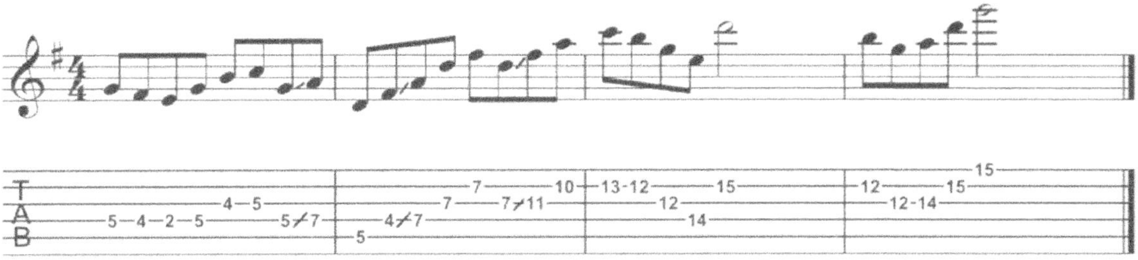

fingering : 4 3 1 4 3 4 3 2 1 2 3 2 1 4 2 1 3 4 2 1 1 2 3

Chapter ELEVEN

Trainings on Key Mode

Section 1   Key Mode and Chords

The 7 types of European key mode scale mentioned previously are actually arranged structures in which the 7 musical notes are allowed individually to be tonics in a natural scale. According to an order of scale, they are respectively Ionian, Dorian, Phrygian, Lydian, Mixolydian, Aeolian and Locrian.

The structure of these 7 key modes is just like a major key and a minor key, taking the names of tonic to name key modes. For instance, Mixolydian key mode which uses E note as a tonic is then E Mixolydian, and Dorian key mode which uses G as a tonic is then G Dorian.

Taking structure as one example, although the structure of each key mode is not the same, you don't need to memorize their scale graphics. And this is because they use a natural scale in the same key mode to form them. Even if you are willing to memorize them, in the end you will discover it is the same graphic, and the only difference is the starting note to be different.

And there's still a lot to talk about key mode. However, it's not in the coverage of this book. If you are interested in such topic, please look for other learning materials.

◆Key Mode and Chords

From scale format we learn that because Dorian, Phrygian and Aeolian have a structure of 1, ^{b}3 and 5, they are often used when a minor third is used as background. And Ionian, Lydian and Mixolydian are often used when background is a major third chord.

Tonic	Mode	Scale	Format (1 refers to tonic)						
C	C Ionian	C D E F G A B	1	2	3	4	5	6	7
D	D Dorian	D E F G A B C	1	2	b3	4	5	6	b7
E	E Phrygian	E F G A B C D	1	b2	b3	4	5	b6	b7
F	F Lydian	F G A B C D E	1	2	3	#4	5	6	7
G	G Mixolydian	G A B C D E F	1	2	3	4	5	6	b7
A	A Aeolian	A B C D E F G	1	2	b3	4	5	b6	b7
B	B Locrian	B C D E F G A	1	b2	b3	4	b5	b6	b7

◆Minor Third Chord

For instance, if the background is a Dm chord, it can match the performance of D Dorian, D Phrygian or D Aeolian. However, if it uses D Dorian, you can think of playing the 2nd note as D in a C key scale to perform. If it uses D Phrygian, you can think of playing the 3rd note as D in a ^{b}B key scale to perform.

This way, you can continue to proceed to choose different scales in different keys to perform while chords are in progression. For instance, it is like you must not stop key modulations for training the changes in scale building blocks, thus this can enhance the familiarity of a fretboard.

<D Dorian>

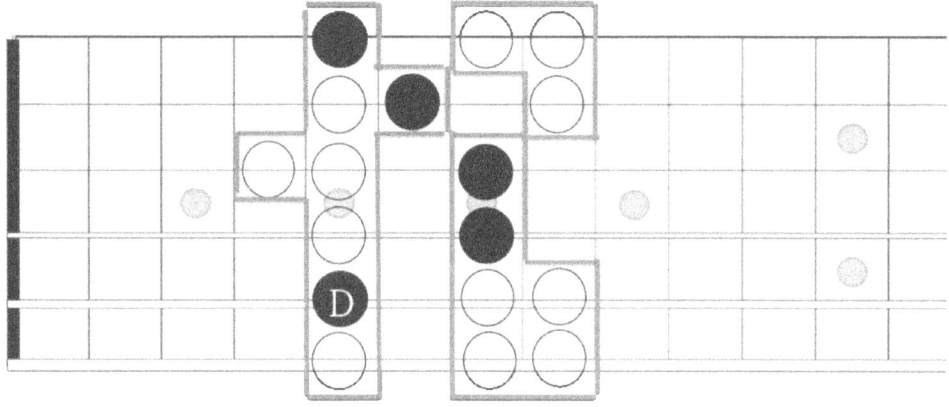

Taking Dm as II in C Major key, D note as the 2nd note to play in C key scale.

<D Phrygian>

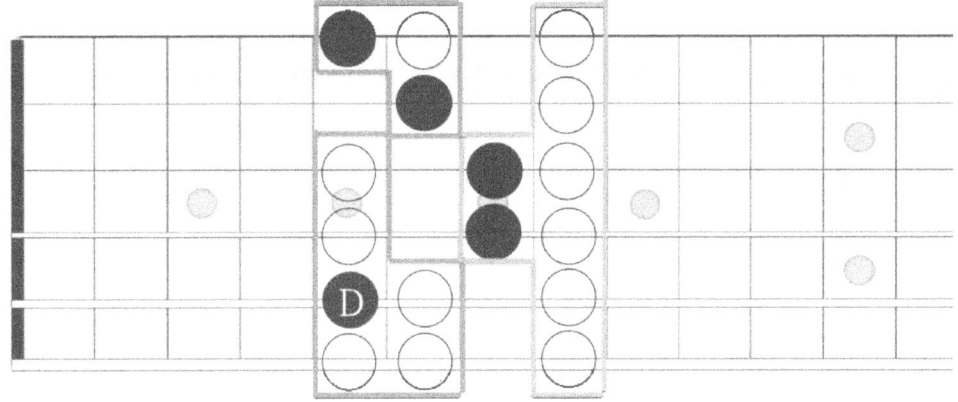

Taking Dm as III in ^{b}B Major key, D note as the 3rd note to play in ^{b}B scale.

<D Aeolian>

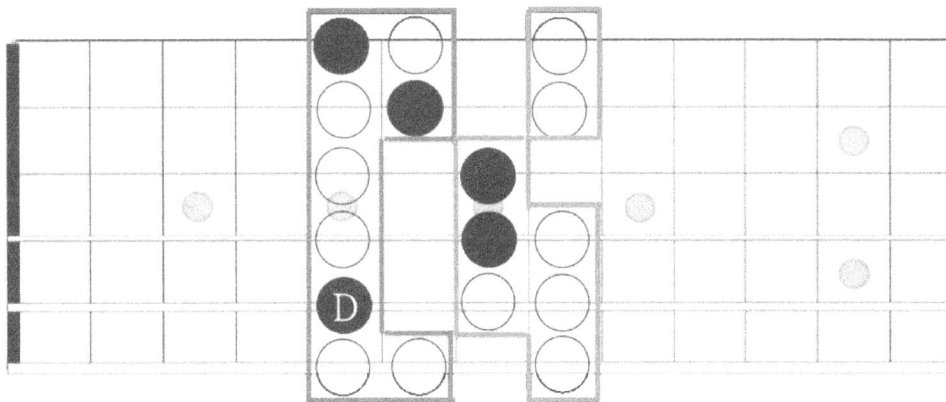

Taking Dm as VI in F Major key, D note as the 6th note to play in F key scale.

♦Major Third Chord

If the background is a G chord, you can match accompanying G Ionian (taking G key scale, 1st note as tonic); G Lydian (D key scale, 4th note as tonic); G Mixolydian (C key scale, 5th note as tonic).

\<G Ionian\>

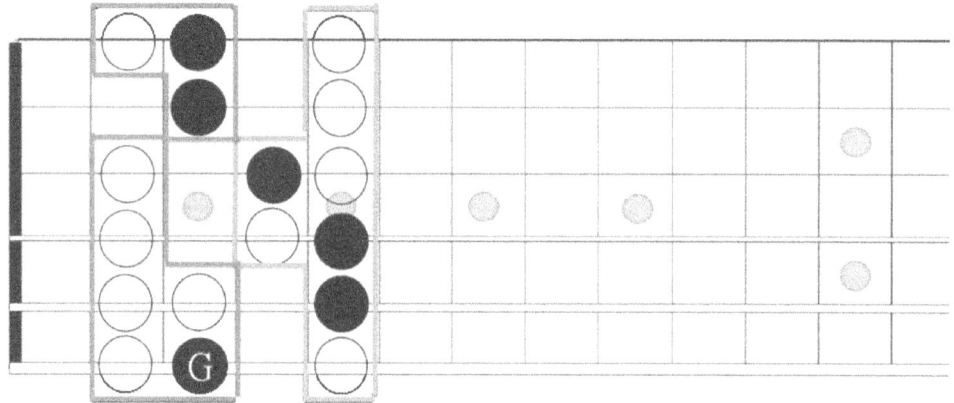

Taking G as I in G Major, G note as the 1st note in G key scale to play.

\<G Lydian\>

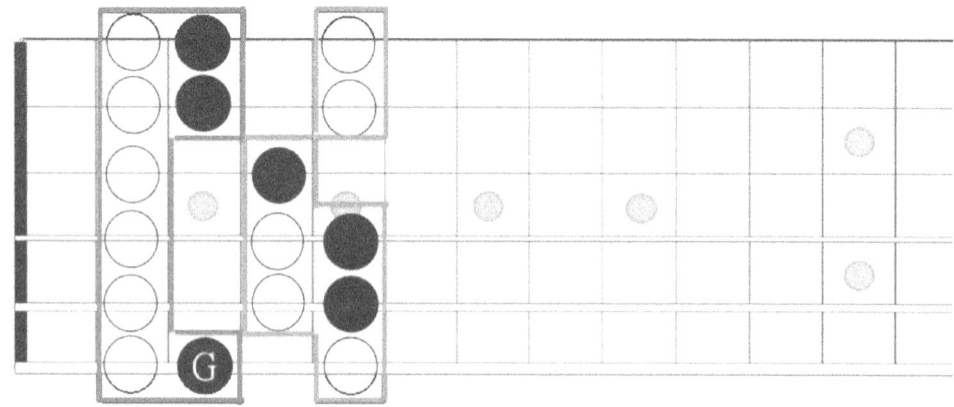

Taking G as IV in D Major, G note as the 4th note in D key scale to play.

<G Mixolydian>

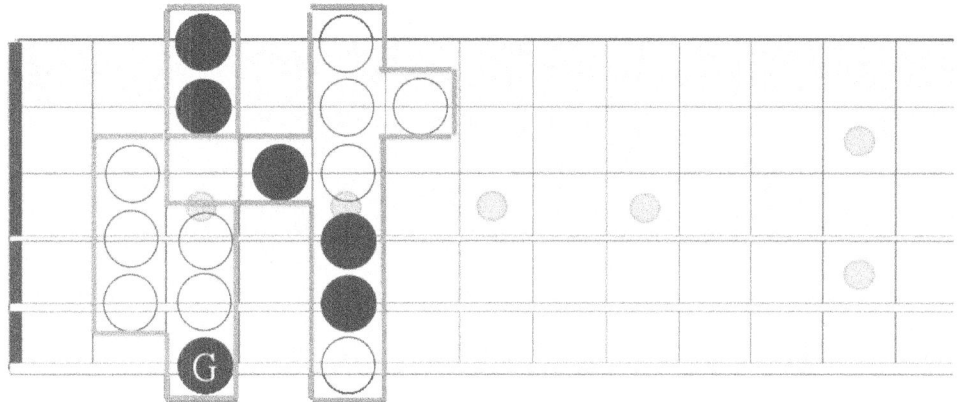

Taking G as V in C Major, G note as the 5th note in C key scale to play.

Analyzing and comparing musical notes of G, C and D keys, then you will discover F note is the only difference in G key and C key. Likewise, it's F$^\#$ in G key, F in C key and others are the same notes. Therefore, there's only one position of musical note for graphics on a fretboard that need changes. However, C note is the only difference in G key and D key, where it's C in G key, C$^\#$ in D key and others are the same notes.

	1	2	3	4	5	6	7
C Major	C	D	E	F	G	A	B
G Major	G	A	B	C	D	E	F#
D Major	D	E	F#	G	A	B	C#

If it's scales of other different keys, there may be more different notes appearing. At this time, if you are planning for a switch then it's a test for your understanding for different note. While conducting a self-training, you may pay attention to the methods below:

1. Start practices from scales which contain fewer different notes

How do you know the different notes in between scales?

The quickest way is taking out the Circle of Fifth and look up to it.

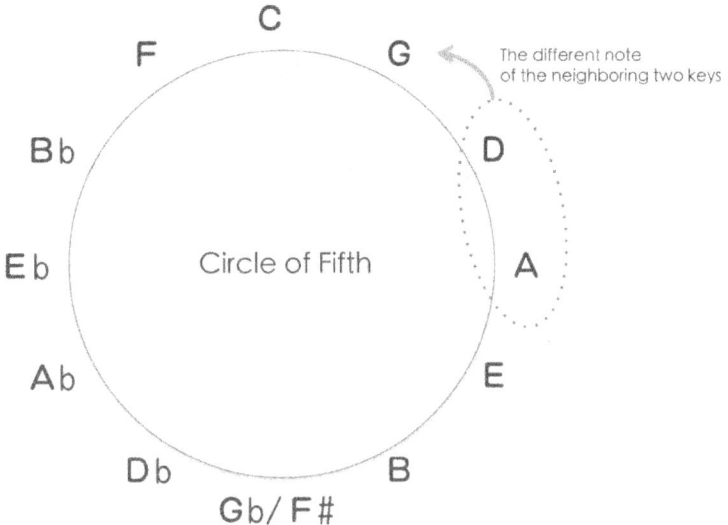

Circle of Fifth

The different note
of the neighboring two keys

In the Circle of Fifth, after choosing a certain key, there is just one different note between neighboring keys of the two sides and the selected scales. And the different note of the neighboring two keys happens to be tonic of the left neighboring key to the further left side key. For instance, in scales of C and G keys, it is the F note to be different. And in scales of D and A keys, the different note is G (G and G$^{\#}$), and the different note for E^{b} and A^{b} keys is D (D and D^{b}).

The number of different note then is based on the separated difference and increase. It is one different note for the neighboring note. One key apart is 2 different notes whereas 2 keys apart are 3 different notes and so on.

2. You can try to do switching upon practices

This way, in addition to apparent changes in aural aspect, it is also suitable for fretboard trainings when encountering key modulations or upon uses of other scales, you can be more familiar with fast reactions.

3. Matching Chord Background for Practices

The most important matter of this part is to use your ears and listen to it. By allowing your ears to get used to changes in background music, what would be the most suitable scales to play and what changes in musical notes would give the best matching tastes. The ultimate goal of this practice method is to allow yourself completely not to care about which keys. Once chords of musical background have changed, you will immediately know what musical notes to play to be suitable next anyways. This is the so called "no method is a good method".

When it appears to be single chords for continuous several measures in music, you can try switching key scale modes for use.

<1> A Chord (Fingering of Open E Chord)

[Track-63]

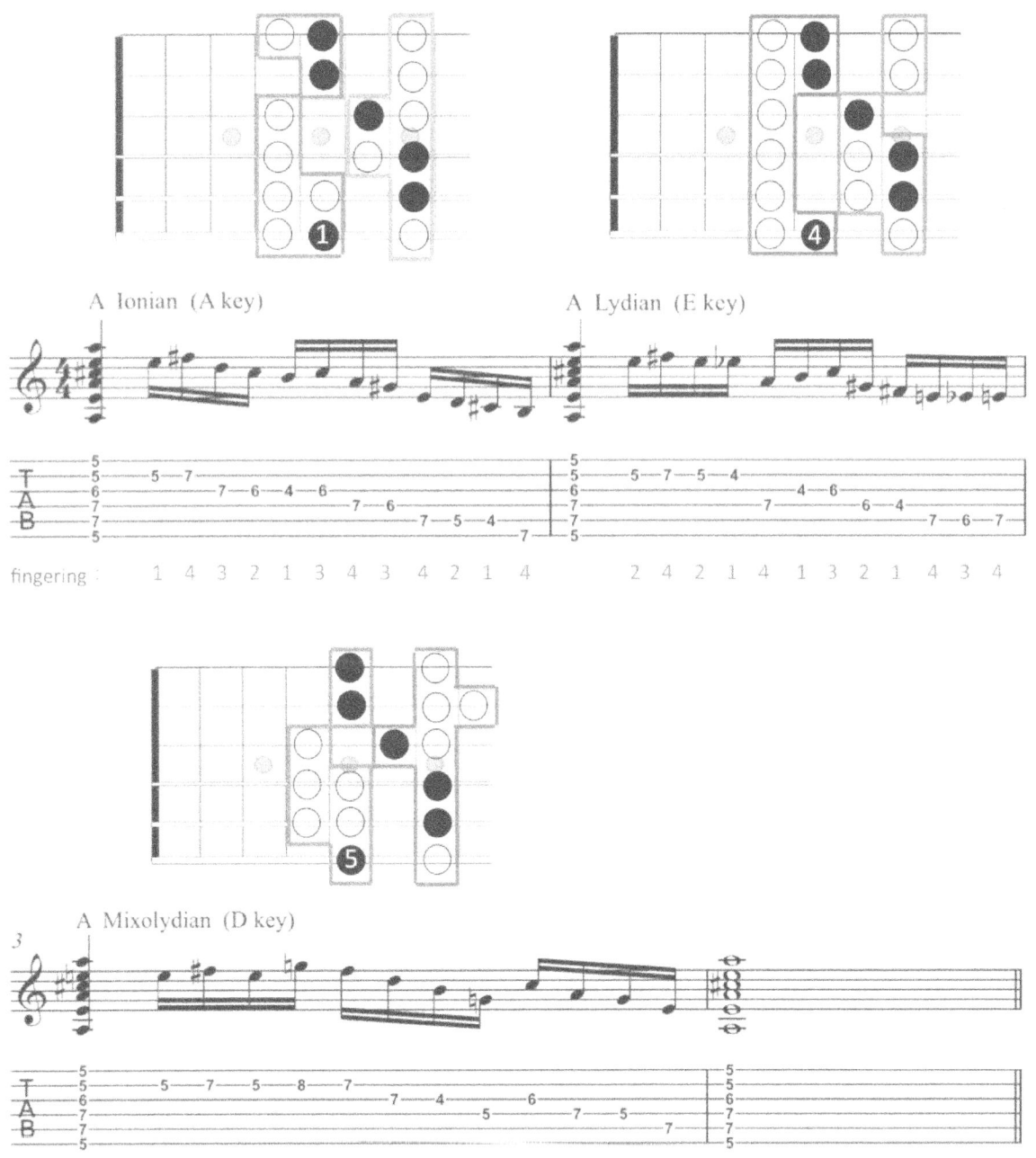

<2> A Chord (Fingering of Open G Chord)

[Track-64]

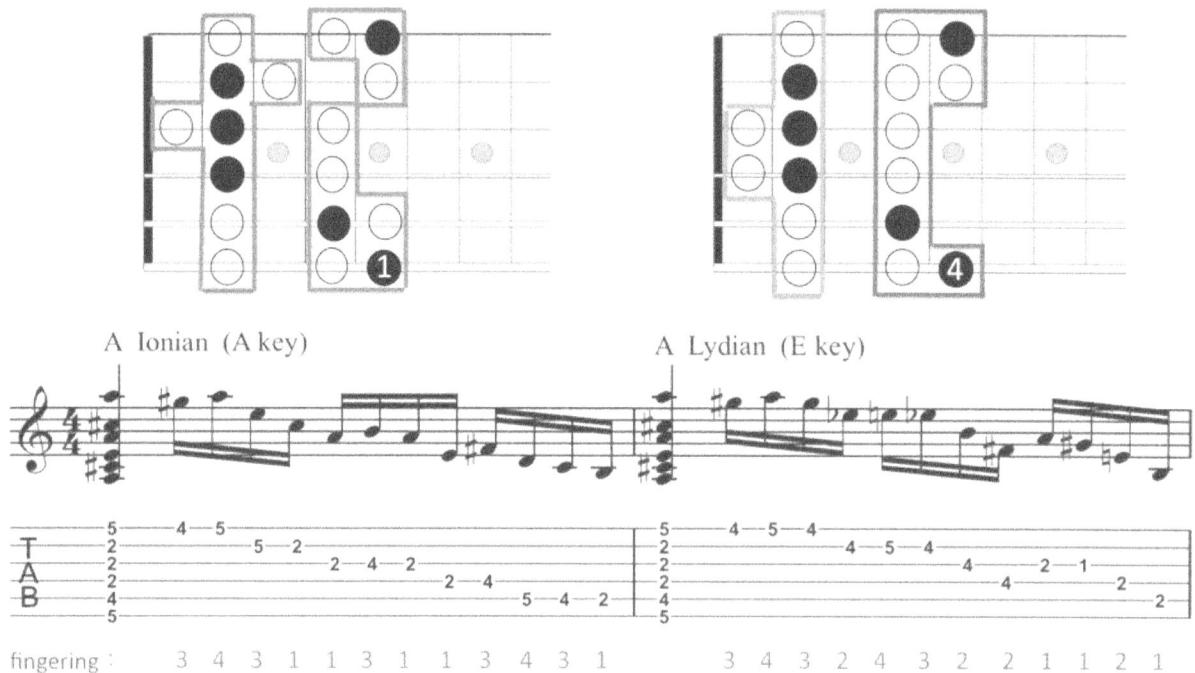

A Ionian (A key)

A Lydian (E key)

fingering : 3 4 3 1 1 3 1 1 3 4 3 1   3 4 3 2 4 3 2 2 1 1 2 1

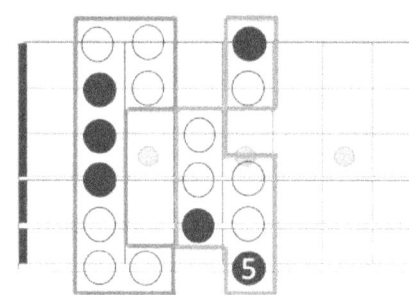

A Mixolydian (D key)

4 3 1 2 1 2 3 4 3 4 3 1

<3> Cm Chord (Fingering of Open Am Chord)

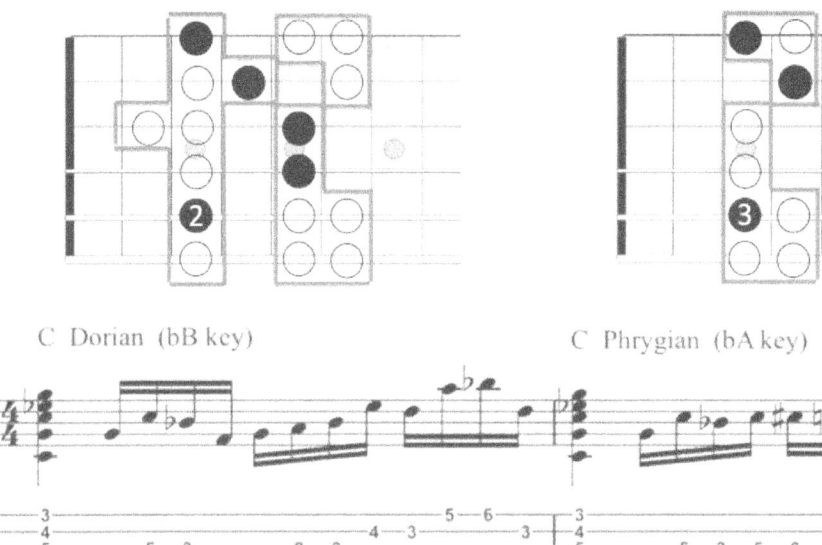

C Dorian (bB key)   C Phrygian (bA key)

fingering :   3 4 1 1 4 1 2 3 1 3 4 1   3 4 1 3 4 3 2 1 2 4 3 1

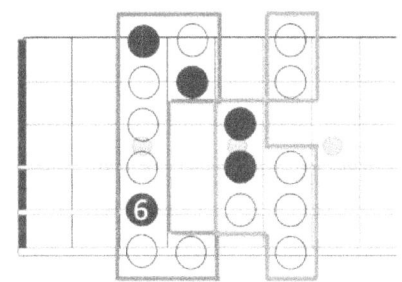

C Aeolian (bE key)

    3 4 1 1 2 1 2 1 2 3 2 3

THE APPLICATIONS : Final, Enhances Practices Everywhere

CONCLUSION : HOW TO PRACTICE

This secret handbook primarily allows you to be gradually familiar with a fretboard via more efficient methods. You then can think about a series of performance movements, develop more and more performance patterns on your own. You can discover more different styles of yours. Although techniques are not of the concerns in this secret handbook, however, technique wise, these mantras can help you be more flexible upon technique use. Performance wise, you would still need sufficient techniques to support your musical ideas and phrases, therefore please don't neglect technique practices.

As for scale building block graphics, I would like to suggest you to make a few more copies of the attached fretboard charts in the back of this handbook. When you wake up in the morning or in any of your spare time, you can take a piece of blank fretboard graphic to draw a scale graphic on your own. Please wait and see until you don't see any problems in drawing positions of those spots, you then can help them mark tonic positions of major and minor scales. And in the end, you can slowly write down the numbered musical notations of scale. In the beginning, you may probably easily forget or make mistakes, however, please do not be upset. You can directly look up to the original graphics or write copies of them, and this will help you remember them.

And please don't forget to do pattern practices for key transpositions.

Before you take out your guitar to practice, you can also take out a scale graphic. Firstly you can think about what patterns you can play on a fretboard, or how to move a fret position on a fretboard. First please make sure your practice goals and then start working and try them, and slowly you will discover your own creative patterns or musical phrases.

When you are doing other practices, such as arpeggios, chords and practices of all kinds of musical phrases, you need to think about which scale building blocks the musical notes which you're playing belong to. As long as you know where you are, you will not get lost when you are improvising. And even what you are playing is not a natural scale, you can return to positions which you expect, not to mention it would be easy and smooth for you at guitar song arrangements.

If you still feel there's doubts and you want to know more or to practice, you can feel free to contact me. Please welcome to my website or Facebook page. You can also visit iTunes and Spotify to search for "Scott Su". You can listen to guitar performance and composition albums which I have published, including electric guitar and wooden guitar as well as other arranged works!

Scott

FRETBOARD SECRET HANDBOOK : Second Edition.

February 20, 2018.

Written by Scott Su

Translated by Lynda Huang

Final Editor: Scott Su

https://scottsu.net/

Published by STC Music

https://www.stc-music.com/

web@stc-music.com

Copyright © 2017 Scott Su

ISBN 978-986-93878-4-2

All rights reserved. No part of this book may be reproduced in any form or by any electronic or mechanical means including information storage and retrieval systems, without permission in writing from the publisher except by a reviewer who may quote brief passages in a review.

www.ingramcontent.com/pod-product-compliance
Lightning Source LLC
Chambersburg PA
CBHW080127150626
46550CB00017B/2741